W9-BGJ-035

GROW LIKE A LOBSTER

PATHSTONE

GROW
LIKE A
LOBSTER

Plan and Prepare for
Extraordinary Business Results

BRONZE
DOOR

JOSHUA DICK

Grow Like a Lobster:
Plan and Prepare for Extraordinary Business Results

Published by Bronze Door Press

Copyright ©2020 Joshua Dick. All rights reserved.

No part of this book may be reproduced in any form or by any mechanical means, including information storage and retrieval systems without permission in writing from the publisher/author, except by a reviewer who may quote passages in a review.

All images, logos, quotes, and trademarks included in this book are subject to use according to trademark and copyright laws of the United States of America.

ISBN: 978-1-7331604-07

BUSINESS / Management

Cover and Interior design by WorkGroup

QUANTITY PURCHASES: Schools, companies, professional groups, clubs, and other organizations may qualify for special terms when ordering quantities of this title. For information: www.growlikealobster.com.

All rights reserved by Joshua Dick and Bronze Door Press
This book is printed in the United States of America.

BRONZE
DOOR

TABLE OF CONTENTS

6   Introduction: A Lobster-like Approach to Business Growth

14 PART ONE: LARVAL — BUILDING OUR BASE
18 Chapter One: Your One Thing
31 Chapter Two: Mission and Values
43 Chapter Three: Think Bigger
56 Chapter Four: Know Your Audience, Part I: Customers
69 Chapter Five: Create a Powerful Brand

82 PART TWO: MATURE ADULT — FISHABLE BUT STABLE
86 Chapter Six: Know Your Audience, Part II: Employees
106 Chapter Seven: Molting Pains: People
116 Chapter Eight: Avoid Waste
127 Chapter Nine: Document Your Job
140 Chapter Ten: Know Your Audience, Part III: Competitors

152 PART THREE: DOMINANT — CAN'T CATCH ME
157 Chapter Eleven: Going Global: Expand Your Markets
168 Chapter Twelve: Molting Pains: Face Your Crisis
180 Chapter Thirteen: Outside Resources
194 Chapter Fourteen: An Exit of Scale

210 EPILOGUE AND ACKNOWLEDGMENTS
212 Epilogue
214 Acknowledgments

216 APPENDICES
218 Appendix A: Urnex Mission and Values
225 Appendix B: Lobster Legs
228 Notes

INTRODUCTION:
A LOBSTER-LIKE APPROACH TO BUSINESS GROWTH

INTRODUCTION

I never imagined joining the family business that my immigrant great-grandfather started way back in 1936. I had another more prestigious route in mind. Eventually, I would get past my misguided presumptuousness and realize that the small family business represented an amazing opportunity from which to build something of my own. In the process, it would allow me to create my personal dream job, work with amazing people, and achieve extraordinary financial success.

Over the next fifteen years after I joined the business, this diverse manufacturing company would be renamed Urnex Brands, Inc., and become a focused, single-minded organization that produced and sold detergents for cleaning coffee machines. During that time, our product sales grew more than 25 times and annual earnings increased by more than 275 times. The company became a global market leader, increased the number of employees seven-fold, and expanded distribution into more than seventy countries around the world.

The results came through a combination of hard work and an unwavering determination to get the most out of every resource and to streamline every element of the business toward a goal of achieving extraordinary success. Driven by a desire for business security, I learned the important lesson of focusing my efforts on one clearly defined but simple goal, and planning and preparing for the achievement of that goal. No one taught me this lesson; I had to learn it along the way.

Business-building can be filled with stomach-churning insecurities, people-management issues, constant tension, and humbling personal introspection. Every day of my career as an entrepreneur, I feared failure. In response, I also came to despise distraction. I developed an approach to moving forward at a constant, consistent, ambitious but also attainable pace that would accept moderated growth in exchange for constant progress.

Somewhere along this journey, as I found and developed simplified models upon which to focus and drive our efforts at Urnex, I discovered the lobster — an unexpected symbol upon which to frame a business message, especially coming from someone in the coffee industry.

I came to see the lobster and its regular and painful process of molting as a metaphor for how any business striving for consistent, controlled, exceptional growth can achieve greatness by managing the ups and preparing for the downs. Just as the mandate to "grow like a lobster" explained throughout this book became the theme of my business life, I hope that exploring strategies and initiatives through this lens can add inspiration and fun to yours. My lobster-based approach is about never looking back, but also never racing forward. It is a no-nonsense, frugal business model that depends on unwavering focus in order to achieve wild success.

THE LOBSTER AS A METAPHOR FOR BUSINESS EVOLUTION

The inspiration for the metaphor came from the agonizing and frequently recurring process a lobster goes through to molt — to shed its old shell, expose its vulnerability, and construct a new, larger one. I give credit to Trevor Corson's The Secret Life of Lobsters for making me aware of this phenomenon in 2005. At the time, I was a few years into my career as an entrepreneur.

Along the way, I had also been through a number of traumatic — what I would later identify as molt-like — experiences. These included protracted union negotiations with the Teamsters, a mis-shipment of several full pallets (rather than a single sample) of product to the corporate office of the buyer at our largest customer (still the world's largest specialty coffee retailer today), a first of two family buyout transactions within the business, the decision to close six diverse product lines which accounted for about 55 percent of revenue, a competitive acquisition, and the impending arrival of my first child. It was then that my pleasure reading of Corson's book led me to this quote referenced in the business diary I had kept from the start:

"A lobster's shell gives the animal all of its rigidity. Under the shell, the lobster is little more than jelly-soft flesh and floppy organs. The problem with this arrangement is that the lobster is constantly growing, while its shell is fixed in size. To get bigger a lobster must literally burst its seams, escape its old shell, and expose its vulnerable inner self to the hungry world while it constructs a new shell large enough to allow its body to expand."[i]

Corson's book led to my mirroring the personal business experiences of strength and stability followed by weakness and vulnerability — similar to what a lobster experiences during each molt. Over the next ten-plus years, I took to frequently talking with my team using the lobster imagery. I would point out situations requiring the need to plan and prepare for the future (*See Chapter Two: Mission and Values*) and the inevitability of regular molts. I found myself reminding our team that while at times our business is strong, at other times it is weak and uncertain. Being aware of these trends seemed to be a step toward personal and business maturity. The lobster image became the anchor for future growth and successful management of many future molts at Urnex.

While our shells are hard and strong, we can go out in the world and seek new business, invest in new technologies, and set up our systems, priorities, and initiatives as we build our base for the future. That's all well and good, but I was more emotionally connected to the concept of the vulnerability that occurs during a molt. I found myself reflecting that imagery onto moments when everything seemed to go wrong. It was during those times when competitors launched a new product that might infringe on our intellectual property, a production machine broke, a labor issue arose, or a winter snowstorm crippled transportation, when it felt like the business had shed its shell and aspiring predators lurked all about, hoping to devour us. It seemed that groups of those terrible experiences happened concurrently — and as they did, the entire organization was able to take them in stride and avoid frantic distraction because we recognized each event as a molt for which we had prepared.

While working on this book, I came to realize that the metaphor of the "molt" is just one of many possible connections between the life of a lobster and the business lessons and experiences gained during my career. The life cycle of a lobster can credibly be connected to the evolution of any business.

A lobster grows consistently throughout its entire life — never stopping. With each molt, its size increases about 15 percent. It never shrinks other than for the brief moments when it squeezes itself together to escape and discard its shell. Immediately after, it quickly expands to fill its new space and awaits the formation of a new shell.

Coincidentally, my goal in business had always been to achieve consistent, conservative, and never-ending topline growth. I never sought growth of more than 15 percent per year, nor expected anything less. I often talked about it as driving a car with two feet, meaning one foot on the accelerator and the other simultaneously on the brake. I know you can't do both at the same time, but the idea is that it moderates velocity. During a fifteen-year career of trying to be conservative and only grow as much as we could handle, the business achieved all fifteen consecutive years of roughly 15 percent topline growth. Compound annual growth for the period was 22.3 percent.

URNEX TOPLINE SALES – PERCENT INCREASE VS. PRIOR YEAR

Consistent, controlled topline growth delivered operational efficiency that led to incredible value creation. When I had achieved certain goals, I deeply contemplated the opportunity to sell the business to private equity investors. When that opportunity materialized, I had a chance to step back and reflect on my experiences and the learning gained during my journey. I realized that my story could serve as a foundation for sharing thoughts, ideas, and philosophies that might help others in their efforts to grow and expand businesses of all types.

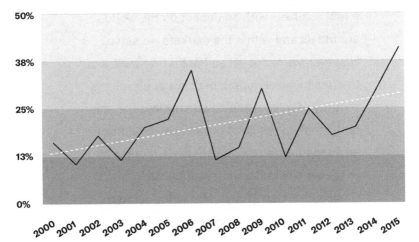

* Dip years were related to sales declines due to the closing of unfocused product lines. Core business growth is represented by the trendline.

While your business's potential rate of growth may vary from what mine experienced, the concepts I share can add value to your thought process and planning. As I set out to tell a story and offer my advice on how to achieve the type of growth and security we created, I recognized that the lobster metaphor I used for all those years had much more to offer. In reading biology texts and interviewing marine biology professors and lobster experts, I started to see that the lifecycle of a lobster mirrors all businesses. In fact, we can think about any business across three stages of development that match the lifecycle of a lobster:

1. Larval — Building Our Base: Our business is young and nimble, enthusiastic and filled with energy. We are growing fast but our scale is still small enough that we can make quick pivots, invest for the future, and learn about ourselves. It is during this time that we set the foundation for the future we envision.

2. Mature Adult — Fishable But Stable: We are a real business with an impact on the world around us and within the markets we serve. However, we're not yet so big that we have lost the freshness of our mindset nor achieved the security of more established entities. The spirit for big risk-taking (and occasional shedding of an appendage/employee) remains, along with the determination to push ourselves forward.

3. Dominant — Can't Catch Me: While we were a real business before, we're now a leader in our industry. We are recognized across all spectrums of our customer base and thinking about growth at a scale that is multiples upon multiples larger than where we began.

On my first day at the business, I had very little idea what I was getting myself into. However, somehow, I knew I was never going to be happy in the corporate world working for others. I also knew I wanted a chance to build something that fit my style and allowed me to work with people who self-selected a similar approach to work and life. In setting out to create my own dream job, I learned that loving one's job provides a chance to make decisions about each phase of business with a unique freedom. I hope I can help you find your own freedom.

Joshua Dick

PART ONE:
LARVAL —
BUILDING
OUR BASE

PART ONE

"From every 50,000 eggs only about two lobsters are expected to survive to legal size," notes the Lobster Institute at the University of Maine.[ii] Over the next few years, those survivors that evade predators and make it through molt after molt must then avoid being caught in the thousands of traps enticingly set near their homes. Should they manage to stay off your dinner table, they continue to molt, propagate, and grow without issue year after year in near perpetuity.

No matter what phase your business is in today, the goal is to move past the start-up or larval phase — and become the equivalent of a mature lobster with a hard, protective shell, able to be secure and free to grow and reproduce — or in your case, able to deliver significant financial returns. Those that make it through each phase of the life cycle, both in marine biology and business evolution, have done so through some fortune, but more often from proper planning, determination, and lots of hard work.

It takes from five to seven years for a lobster to grow to a size large enough for legal harvest. During this early stage of life, a lobster may molt as many as twenty-five times. In a new business, the juvenile/larval phase is a time to grow and develop, stabilize, and streamline. We can make incremental investments and developments in thinking about who we are and what we want to be.

In these stages of a business, we have a chance to invest for the future that we expect to build. Later, change becomes more complicated as we are no longer as agile and nimble. The foundational steps we take toward self-awareness are key to our future success. In Part I of this book, I'll guide you in building the basis of a future organization. Chapters One through Five cover topics such as identifying your One Thing, defining your core identity through mission and values statements, projecting your business at the scale you aspire to achieve, recognizing your audience, and brand building. Let's get into it.

CHAPTER ONE

YOUR ONE THING

It all started with my great-grandfather who was an immigrant tailor. He took the bold step of coming to the United States to escape conscription in the Austrian army in the early 1900s. In 1936, he started a textile and sewing company on the Lower East Side of Manhattan. Over the years, he found his living making many different types of simple, sewn items, from hat covers to pillowcases ... anything that would pay the bills and allow him personal security. He raised his family in an apartment above his sewing shop. Eventually, his son (my grandfather) and grandson (my father) would find their ways into the business; each adapted and adjusted it to the market opportunities they detected. They built a stable entity that provided a comfortable lifestyle, and worked diligently to find safety and avoid vulnerability so they would be free to enjoy other parts of life.

Among the many varied textile items the company produced in booming post-WWII New York were cloth filters for brewing coffee. At some point in the 1940s, my great-grandfather learned that keeping a coffee machine clean was the key to a roaster maintaining its wholesale accounts. As the story goes, the coffee suppliers would collect glass decanters from diners and restaurants each week, and bring them back to the roasteries to be cleaned. If they failed to clean the serving vessels, the taste of the coffee became bitter from contact with rancid old coffee oil residue — resulting in angry or suspicious customers wondering if they had purchased coffee with compromised quality.

With that, the family business broadened its portfolio from sewing to offering one chemical detergent for cleaning coffee equipment. While this opportunistic product launch would become the foundation of the business I went on to build, the company continued to follow other opportunities in a way that led to distraction and uncertainty. By the time I joined, a portfolio of seven diverse product lines — each unable to support the business independently — kept our business both stagnant and overextended. It was my frustration with the inefficiency of managing each product line just to keep the whole boat afloat that led me to determine to focus all my resources on being the best at One Thing and One Thing only. I would never allow the business or myself to be distracted again.

Over a span of sixty-plus years, the business had continued to follow each opportunity as it arose, exchanging sales in one area for those in another, yet never really increasing the size of the whole. In reflection, it must have been an exhausting but exciting process. When I joined, the business was segmented into very loosely related product lines. Items included coffee cleaners, filter bags and brushes, lemon covers, pastry bags, and of all things, shellfish steamer bags (perfect for a lobster boil), knit material, tube tops, hat covers, and party supply accessories and textiles.

In the 1960s, the business introduced a lemon wedge bag[1] when a family member realized that the existing sewing machines could make these little bags for keeping lemon pits contained. In the 1970s, the business entered the world of tube tops — yes, those elasticized terry cloth articles of clothing that seem to protect a woman's breasts from exposure ever so precariously. They were sort of like a one-size-fits-all giant wristband for your body. If that doesn't say we had strayed from focusing on One Thing, I don't know what does! In many ways, it may have been the extreme diversity and lack of focus across this range of products that led me to overcompensate and bring my focus to the extreme of determination on avoiding the painful distractions I observed.

PRODUCT LINES – PERCENT SALES

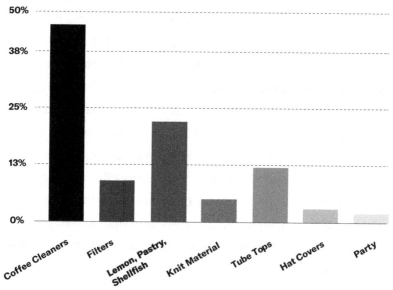

For each decision the business owners made to go into this

---

1 Gauze cloth covers used to prevent the release of pits when squeezing a lemon.

ever-diverse group of products, they had a rationale that seemed perfectly clear. These were business decisions or temptations that every organization faces daily. For example, there are times when an existing customer asks for a new product that is outside your skill set, or a contact you hope to please happens to need someone to assemble something — and since you have labor on staff, you decide to give it a try. Getting distracted is not a mass movement or a decision to purposely fragment your business. It is a slow, subconscious activity that permeates a business when you just want to take advantage of opportunities and be a good partner.

Later in the book, we will revisit the deep importance of satisfying the customer; however, you have to do this without sacrificing your own success. Knowing when to say no and having the courage to do so is a big step toward professional maturity. By allowing oneself to be randomly opportunistic, one risks losing focus and therefore sacrificing an ability to serve the customers that matter most. In the case of my family's business, sales were declining, key customers were leaving, and most importantly, no one was secure.

My determination to focus on One Thing came as a direct response to the situation I joined. Over the previous years, the business had evolved into a diversified collection of unrelated product lines, and its owners accepted the satisfaction of low-risk stability in exchange for a less certain chance of exceptional success. It was my frustration with the inefficiency of diversification that became the foundation of my vision for how to harden your business shell and achieve extraordinary results.

Before I can get to how my changes to the family business can be of value to you, I have to get something out of the way. Yes, I started working at a family business, and yes, I was very, very fortunate that three generations before me had created a legacy upon which I was able to dedicate my efforts. It is very important to me to separate my ego from business decision-making — remember that my ego almost kept me from getting involved with the family business in the first place. Yet, when it comes to talking about the fact that I "sold my family business" — I am uncomfortable. I struggle with how to present the story of the business in a way that is both accurate and respectful. I am deeply grateful for the work that was done to establish the business before I got involved and for the opportunity to build upon those efforts. For five years after my father left the business, my brother was also my partner and an equal shareholder. He was an intimate part of the early years and he contributed greatly to building the base of later success. After my brother left the company, I began to think differently. I knew that I had a special opportunity. I hope that what I did with the opportunity and how my team and I focused our resources will be of value to you.

At this point, I want to share the first of several statements relevant to the topic at hand I call "lobster legs" that you'll see throughout the book. Each is highlighted in italics and repeated at the ends of the chapters. Think of these legs as the supports and anchors of strength that hold up a lobster. They are intended to provide concepts for you to take away and reflect on from each chapter. Here's the first one: *Focus is the key. Simplified focus is the path to consistent, controlled growth and security.*

LIFE AS A BUSINESS LOBSTER

When we look at the variety of life in the ocean, we may not realize that — like businesses that need a niche in which to thrive and to dedicate resources — the number and type of animals that can be sustained in an aquatic environment depends on the animals finding safe homes where they can mate, find food, and allow their young to mature. Every lobster seeks out a shelter of appropriate size to secure itself from predators — a protection particularly important just after molt. The determined focus of the lobster to find a perfect shelter in what feels like an oceanic game of musical chairs is the same philosophy one needs to adopt in order to succeed in building a successful organization and enterprise. You owe it to yourself to commit to focusing on where you want your business to be positioned — to find what I call your One Thing and stick with it in times of strength when your shell glistens brilliantly in the waves, and in times of weakness when you've just molted and have become vulnerable.

To refer again to Corson's book, *The Secret Life of Lobsters:* "Lobsters (are) partial to a home with an escape hatch — an exit in the back that was small enough not to require constant defending, but that allowed the lobster to slip out in an emergency."[iii] I know it's the first but it is also the only place I will advocate that you not behave like a lobster, but do the opposite. I believe strongly that an escape hatch is a bad idea for a business that wants to achieve something special. Picking a cave with a second exit in the back is a perfect way to lose focus and allow oneself to be distracted — were tube tops really a fit with coffee cleaning products and lemon covers?

Find the right cave and you won't need an escape plan. It was with this base that I adopted this concept: *Don't give yourself a chance to fail and certainly don't leave yourself an escape hatch.* Never allow yourself a crutch. Be confident in your abilities. After you have found and developed ideas that you believe in, go toward them with a conviction that you will never need the escape hatch.

To some, this is a bit of an alarming concept, as it seems like I'm telling you to put all your eggs in one basket. Of course, I'm not suggesting you go all-in on day one. First, you take the time to assess your business, your market, your team, your outside suppliers, and your other resources. Next, you make commitments and get things focused. You need to know yourself and your own capabilities and make firm decisions about where you want to go and what you want to achieve. In my case, the determined focus I found was a direct response to my frustration with the disjointed nature of the business I joined. I had a visceral reaction to the difficulty imposed on the business by its lack of focus, and I set out to do One Thing really well, set clear goals, and never let myself fall into the trap of reactiveness.

When you operate a business always thinking you are protecting yourself by extending into new and unfocused ventures, you run the risk of over-diversifying in a way that will thin out your attention and prevent you from growing. You must ask yourself as honestly as possible: Is your business large enough to need to be diversified? Do you have the time, bandwidth, or human resources to try to do more than One Thing at the level of excellence to which you aspire? If you try to find your escape hatch by expanding and changing your business into a set of complementary security blankets, you risk muddling through the operation without a clear objective and plan. This probably isn't an earthshaking concept, but we all get distracted, and being aware of the risks of distraction gives us a chance to self-reflect and refocus when needed.

SIMPLIFYING WITH FOCUS

The opposite of over-diversifying is what I call "simplifying with focus." Throughout this book, you will find examples of concepts I simplified and prioritized in a way that you could implement them. Who has the time or patience to overcomplicate things? While I was dealing with an organization already spread thin, you may be starting from scratch and not quite sure where to dedicate your efforts. Work hard to avoid spreading yourself wide before you have a chance to find your focus. Unplanned diversification leaves you stagnating in a shell that can't expand, and doomed to a life without exceptional growth.

While beginning any effort to find a focus, step one is to assess what is going on with each product line or what options are in front of you. In my case, I had to ask why we were even selling certain items that were losing money or sold in small quantities. What gaps existed?

Knowing your business means monitoring and analyzing the time spent on customer support, sales, and operations on each product line, and measuring sales and profitability of each item across all the costs — direct and indirect. Don't deceive yourself. You need to monitor even the smallest products. I developed a simple daily tracking page to provide a quick look at each key area of the business, including sales, costs, and unquantifiable expenses. You must commit to knowing each element of the business personally. It is humbling to analyze and collect data yourself, but you'll never reach a point where you are free of these responsibilities if you don't accept them in the beginning. Remember, the goal here is to build a business that can exist on its own and to build something beyond the ordinary. You want extraordinary results. To get there, you must start by understanding and interacting intimately with the numbers, the people, the operations, and the customers. How close are you to the details of your business? Close enough?

MY ONE THING

As I started analyzing profitability, distribution, and the overall potential of each product line, I realized that the little coffee machine cleaning product called Urn Cleaner had a sort of glimmer to it. I saw it as "ownable" and "scalable." With this, I mean it was protectable and able to grow and iterate on its own.

As we will cover in Chapter Five on building a brand, a business's viability is directly tied to its uniqueness and audience appeal.

What I saw in the Urn Cleaner product was a way to connect to an industry. Many people around the world start their day with coffee. While I didn't know much about the beverage before entering the industry, I was aware that it was an important lifestyle product. If the NBC TV network could dedicate an entire show to a group of six young adults hanging out in a coffee shop (*Friends*), I sensed that an opportunity to connect to this very personal industry was worthy of additional thought.

While step one was studying the business, which led to recognizing the potential of the coffee machine cleaning product line, step two was making sure I wasn't rushing. I continued to look at the other product lines that I hadn't found as valuable. These items were, in fact, more than 50 percent of our sales, and I was immediately ready to shut them all down. *Going too fast has just as many risks as going too slowly.*

I have a lot of respect for my father, and I know that since he had been investing time and money in certain products, he had good reasons. The textile-related products provided sustainable profit and operating income, and that is what I'm sure attracted him to those businesses. However, I later decided that they could all be copied by someone else. They had no brand identity and therefore nothing to hang onto and build upon.

While I saw chances to grow some parts of these product lines to increase their scale, I also realized that they were deeply vulnerable to outsourced manufacturing and price-based competition. If just about anyone could make these things, we would have no advantage that was discernible. Later on, I talk about the value of finding a boring, unsexy product or business area to develop. One might say that I had an embarrassment of riches in the department of boring product lines to choose from. In the end, the really big, bold step was in finding the courage to walk away from the profitable but limited business lines in order to find my One Thing and get on a different path. Do you have parts of your business you should let go? Are there new businesses you are thinking of getting into that don't fit?

With coffee machine cleaners, I found something that people connected to, and I was determined to focus on it above all else. It was still a pretty boring space and product concept, but the product had a brand name, "Urnex," and despite being one small, low-margin product only used to clean coffee machines, people knew it in the coffee industry.

As we will see in *Chapter Four: Know Your Audience: Customers,* immersing yourself in the market is the best way to gain an understanding of your audience, and finding things your audience wants or needs is a way to achieve premium pricing. I found that those who knew Urnex had developed an emotional attachment to the brand. Some remembered using it while working in the kitchen during summer breaks or cleaning coffee machines in the dining hall while working their way through college. On more than a few occasions, I heard the word Urnex used as a verb. The first time someone talked about the need "to Urnex" his coffee machine as the key to great coffee, I felt like I had found my shelter or my One Thing, and the place I was going to dedicate myself and my focus. Everything else would have to go.

TIME TO DIVEST

Despite the financial security provided by the six other product lines in the portfolio, which represented over 50 percent of the sales and more of the profit, I determined to close them all and focus on being great at cleaning coffee machines. I was simplifying the business in order to focus on One Thing. The project of closing those product lines would consume the next five years and in effect represent the many small molts common in the first five to seven years of the life of a lobster. This was a time that I split my bandwidth and that of the organization between selling and closing these other product lines, and setting up the coffee machine cleaning business as our only focus and base. Focus became our motto and we were determined not to let anything distract us. Is there anything you should be cutting out of your business? If your One Thing isn't really One Thing and you have too many escape hatches and too many distractions, you'll never find a way to move forward at scale.

To do One Thing really well, you need to give yourself a place where you can commit and focus. It doesn't matter what it is that your business does well. The coffee industry simply became my vehicle; these same ideas can be applied to your industry. In fact, these same ideas have been applied by great companies for generations.

Throughout my business education, I was exposed to the philosophies espoused within the great businesses you read about in texts, from companies like Procter & Gamble (P&G), General Electric (GE), and Johnson and Johnson (J&J). I had also worked at Unilever and Salomon Brothers, where I saw major consumer product and investment banking giants lead their industries. These great companies rely on corporate tenets and philosophies to make many internal decisions. Some desire to be either No. 1 or No. 2 in their markets with any product they sell, or they will simply get out of those businesses. Some companies are okay having brands that are not the top of their category — and they still make these profitable. The focus doesn't matter as much as having a focus and committing to it. Great companies — big and small — know who they are and are focused on achieving their objectives without any distractions. In the case of Urnex, we decided we wanted our One Thing to be supporting the coffee industry and becoming an indispensable partner to that community's growth.

FIND A BORING SPACE TO FOCUS YOUR ENERGIES

There was a time in history when lobsters were so prevalent along the coasts of North America that they were considered prison food. Can you imagine? The incarcerated were essentially experiencing today's finest dining and then returning to their cellblocks. At times, lobsters would wash up on New England coasts by the thousands, and their carcasses were used to fertilize fields and feed animals. Their meat was unappreciated, unnoticed as delicious, and due to its easy availability, simply ignored. No one wanted anything to do with the lobster.

To me, the best business is the one no one is interested in. We're not talking about commodity products, but ones that no one cares about. Find me a product or a space that has a value and a unique benefit to offer, yet everyone ignores, and I'm ready to get to work and focus on it.

During business school, I was struck by a number of key concepts. One first came to me during an entrepreneurship class at Kellogg taught by Professor Steven Rogers. Professor Rogers talked about the path to success through finding the most boring, most unsexy, sleepiest industry one could, and figuring out how to develop it and grow it. In his case, prior to becoming a professor of entrepreneurship, he bought, developed, and sold a business no less boring than a lampshade company. Perfectly uninteresting.

Years later, I was blessed with a whole corral of less than dynamic product lines to choose from. While coffee machine cleaning may have been the most attractive, it only attained that significance through comparison to the rest of the portfolio. I wasn't entering the specialty coffee world of Starbucks and Peet's as a store developer, designing high-end home or commercial brewing equipment for sale at Williams-Sonoma, or traveling the globe sourcing the finest coffee beans in Central America or Africa. I was making soap! It was nearly perfect in its "un-sexiness," along with commercial adhesives, lampshades, or laundromats.

Being in a boring space gave me a chance to assess the opportunities, experiment, and carefully step through my growth objectives. It meant there were fewer competitive distractions. Less attention means more time and room to grow. In essence, I'd found a space that no one else was really thinking about strategically. If pursued carefully, I realized we could have our shelter and our One Thing all to ourselves.

The ocean floor provides enough shelters for millions of lobsters to grow to maturity, provided they find the appropriate space to grow and molt, safe from danger. To find these shelters, lobsters survey the ocean floor carefully and select the perfect spot that fits their identity. As business leaders, we have to select our business objectives just as carefully, find the best markets for our products, and define our focus and targets. We have to laser-tune ourselves on One Thing we can do well and commit ourselves to success.

- **Focus is the key. Simplified focus is the path to consistent, controlled growth and security.**
- **Don't give yourself a chance to fail and certainly don't leave yourself an escape hatch.**
- **Going too fast has just as many risks as going too slowly.**

CHAPTER TWO

MISSION AND VALUES

When a lobster molts, it discards its hard shell so it can build an entirely new and larger one. But while the shell is gone, what remains is the fleshy, core essence of the creature. Its soft body is exposed and vulnerable. Without an exoskeleton, the internal organs and features stay true to the original form and shape and represent the identity of the lobster perpetually. This is the part of the lobster that never goes away — the foundation and framework for each new shell that hardens around it. Over and over again, the lobster remakes itself in the same image — each time a little larger — but its core identity remains the same.

Like lobsters, businesses grow and expand. If you have selectively focused on One Thing, you never need to dramatically change the internal components of your business. Our mission and values define and articulate who we are and where we are going. That core identity points the way to move forward from every challenge. In the long run, the core identity of a business, as expressed in the mission and values statement, is what leads to the irrepressible yet controlled growth we aspire to achieve.

Knowing your core identity and focusing on it with intensity is a source of security; it provides direction and helps you avoid distraction along the way. Confident businesses have an understanding of where they want to allocate their resources, but also have enough confidence to know what areas they are willing to stay away from. Closing profitable business lines that don't fit your plan or turning down a new opportunity because it is clearly outside your strategy takes tremendous discipline. *Saying "no" may be more important than saying yes.*

You might be thinking that mission and values statements are a waste of time. I will agree with you if you plan only to create these documents, but not to use or believe in them. Having worked within a business that lacked a clear understanding of its mission and values allowed me to experience the problems too much freedom and fungibility can create. You may be saying that freedom is what entrepreneurship is about and it's why you love being in business on your own. While that is partly true, how many really successful entrepreneurs who build enduring and extraordinary companies continue to just "wing it" after the first few years? The really good ones take the time to put their plans in place and define their targets. While you may be an entrepreneur because you detest structure, adding the right structure to your business is the only way you are going to achieve something special. In some ways, it was the experience of working in a business with too many unfocused product lines that led me to the epiphany that I needed to close all but one. Take a minute to reflect on your business and how many demands on your resources are outside of your core mission — if you have one.

You may think you don't have the time or energy to sit in a room and write some statement that will get stuck up on a wall or printed on the back of business cards. Regardless of your size, this is not busywork or something left for the consultants to handle. Long ago, I read Jim Collins and Jerry Porras's book *Built to Last* and I was inspired. I came away wanting to create a business that would last (without me) and it seemed that having a well-developed and properly internalized mission statement was a step I couldn't afford to skip. Today, I won't even consider investing in an established company that can't clearly articulate its mission and values statements and explain its One Thing to me.

When it comes to figuring out your focus, you can get stuck trying to follow the rules of every business book you've read, and never accomplish anything. You can also write a polished and business-speakish mission that has nothing personal tying it to you. Here's a little exercise. If you already have a mission statement, take it out of your desk and read it out loud. Now ask yourself if you changed the company name on the header from that of your company to one in another industry (IBM or Ford or Heineken or Nike), would it be obvious that it was your document? Too often, businesses write mission and values statements that are generic and have no true connection to personal identity. If this is what you have, keep reading.

Mission and values statements do not exist so you can just check a box. They are both a path to self-discovery and self-awareness and of foundational importance. They keep you and your organization focused and dedicated to your goals, whether they be consistent and controlled growth, or other aims.

You may be taking over an organization that has a lot of challenges already, or you may be starting from scratch. Regardless of your status, if you are having trouble organizing and implementing simple processes and procedures, then it is essential to take time off to define your base. As you will see further in *Chapter Eight: Avoid*

Waste, I hate waste. I would not tell you to stop and do this if I did not consider it imperative. I only like to dedicate effort to creating something that is of use and that will deliver value. Just writing ideas down and spending a day off-site isn't my thing. We only do stuff if it makes us money. *Wasting time is a waste of time.* Later on, you will see how the work you do in these early stages of business pays dividends when you reach a larger scale. You need a set of rules and a foundation upon which to make decisions and guide prioritization. Without these, you will have a hard time internalizing your core identity.

CRAFTING MISSION AND VALUES STATEMENTS

First of all, what is the difference between a mission statement and a values statement? Put briefly, a mission statement focuses on what you do, and a values statement describes how you are going to do it in a way that works for you. To create the simplest forms of these documents, you can start by listing five or six things under each header that you feel describe your business's inner core identity. You're not done yet, but putting words on paper to go back and reflect on is a major first step.

For the mission statement, you are trying to express the objective of your business — your One Thing — in a way that is broad enough to allow your business to grow and evolve and refocus over the foreseeable (and unforeseeable) future, but not so soft and vague that it will never give you enough direction to say "no" to something. You must ask yourself questions like:

- What is it that I want this business to be or accomplish?
- What defines me/us?
- What do we do well?
- How do we want others to perceive this business?

- What are the rules and guidelines we will follow
  when making a business decision or selecting which
  of two diverse opportunities is best to pursue?
- How do we know which road is the right
  one for our business to follow?

For the values statement, many individuals feel it is paradoxical to speak about the values of a business. A business's reason for existence is to make money, and this logic sometimes suggests that moral or ethical values are out of place in such a discussion. As a result, a values statement can seem forced and hokey, but I advocate instead that you own your own values first and get comfortable expressing them through your business. When it comes to your values, make sure they are ideas that are core to you — don't list environmental responsibility if that's not your thing. Really think about what matters to you. Reflect on the places you've been or organizations you have interacted with that made you happy or impressed you. What was it that made those businesses special? What were their values and how do they compare to your own? While going through this exercise, it is important to recognize that you're not only building a business, you are creating your own dream job, and if you achieve great success, you will have also created the work environment for many others you will hire in the future. As a result, the values have to fit your own identity. Don't list a value to make someone else happy. Make it your own. You can ask questions like:

- What are the things that motivate me and
  should motivate my team and my customers?
- How important is it to me to relate to my customers as
  partners, or are they just contacts that buy from me?
  (It's okay if the latter is how you feel — be honest.)

- What is important to me in terms of loyalty, communication, service, and exposure?
- What makes me happy?
- How would I describe my ethical philosophy?
- How do I think about problem-solving and can that process be useful to the organization?

The key to these documents is that they are focused enough to have true usefulness, but not so tight that they keep you from making decisions or pursuing opportunities that are sometimes a matter of common sense. As an undergraduate, I took a constitutional law class as part of a political science major. While I had been exposed to the US Constitution before, this class helped me develop a deep appreciation for the Constitution as an anchor for political and legal decision-making.

Of course, the Constitution is always interpreted and reinterpreted based on the judicial perspective of the times. Many activities that are legal under today's Constitution would not have been possible interpretations two hundred years ago. In a similar way, you can think of mission and values statements as a business's constitution. It is the document that you look to for tough decisions, wise words you can interpret without losing the core meaning. The mission and values statements are documents that can be changed, of course, but only after deep respect has been paid to the existing document. If you think about how hard it is to pass an Amendment to the US Constitution, you get some sense of how hard it should be to amend these documents of yours. At the same time, if your mission statement is written in a way that you have to constantly pass on great opportunities, or alternatively, if it allows you to justify decisions that have no connection to your One Thing, then something is wrong.

In fact, in all the years of reviewing our mission and values statements, which I tried to do annually or more frequently, our team only ever added two additional words — "Avoid waste" — to the values statement. This addition came at a time when we were implementing a number of environmental and operational initiatives and found that the mission and values statements (which we referenced before taking action) did not make it clear that these efforts were a fit with our core. Other than that, what we started with never changed.

A SAMPLE MISSION AND VALUES STATEMENT

In early February 2001, I had a 100 percent rupture of my Achilles tendon on the squash court. We were midway through the last of five games after splitting the first four games. The score of Game Five was 5–4 in my favor (yes, I remember this precisely) when I lunged for the ball, and my opponent and I both heard a pop. The next day I was on the operating table, and for the next two weeks I was drugged up and bedridden. It was during the post-Percocet[2] downtime when the pain had dissipated and my mind was clear again but I still couldn't walk or drive (call it a molt) that I read and re-read the steps to writing mission and values statements in different books, and even revisited class notes from business school.

I spent a few days working out these statements with my brother, who was also working with me at that time. We talked about every element of the document, and in doing it together, we "owned" it in a way that made it difficult to ever question its value. We were such a small organization then, so Jason and I were able to sit and work on this document by ourselves. We were the assumed successors to the business and we wrote it on our own. However, once it was completed, we gathered our small crew of fourteen people and shared

---

2 Acetaminophen/oxycodone painkiller prescribed post-operatively.

the concepts publicly. We solicited feedback in hopes of bringing everyone into the fold. That document we created fifteen years earlier was the same one in use the day I transitioned out of the CEO role.

This document became the foundation of company outings, and what we referred to when thinking about a tough decision or a new opportunity. Often, employees would have questions about prioritization of their efforts, and we'd look to the mission statement for guidance on where to focus. This was the document I talked with recruits about in interviews, and the document I started off discussing with every new hire. It was the document highlighted when we had a problem or when we had a great success.

Over and over, I showed our team that these few lines were the foundation of our business, and looking to them helped us stay focused and avoid mistakes. Each time a tough situation came up, we could refer to a line or a phrase excerpted from the mission and values statements and make a point or discover the right answer.

In some ways, it can be like a living, always-present coach or advisor to keep you on track. Hopefully, having a look at the Urnex document will help you craft your own such statements. Remember, to do this takes time and thought and effort, and you won't see the benefits of them right away. It's one of those investments we make that we forget about, but if we do it well, it becomes an internalized part of our essence. Following are the mission and values statements upon which Urnex was built into an organization of significant value. In Appendix A, you can see a line-by-line breakdown of the mindset behind each statement and how each was used to manage the business over the years.

MISSION: OBJECTIVE OF YOUR BUSINESS — (WHAT YOU ARE GOING TO DO)

- To make and sell products that fill specialty market needs.
- To offer quality products that satisfy and impress customers.
- To deliver customers the opportunity to enjoy high resale margins.
- To offer employees an attractive lifestyle opportunity.
- To be profitable above and beyond conventional measures.

VALUES — WHAT IS IMPORTANT TO YOUR BUSINESS AND YOUR ORGANIZATION (HOW YOU ARE GOING TO DO IT)

- Act with honesty, integrity, reliability, and consideration for people and the world.
- Serve our customers as we would like to be served.
- Communicate above expectations.
- Plan and prepare for the future.
- Deliver value for shareholders, employees, customers, and the community.
- Avoid waste. (Added 2008)

STEPS TO DOING IT: MISSION AND VALUES STATEMENTS

Okay, so those are the mission and values statements that Urnex used, and if you read the detailed explanations in Appendix A, you will have a sense of our thought processes when we created them. Having mission and values statements is indisputably important. With that said, it's pretty hard to find a document or a plan for how to create them. You are going to have to create your own statement and really think about it. Here are a few suggested steps to get you started:

1. If you are the CEO and/or owner, start a draft of the document on your own. Figure out what you want it to say before getting others involved. Develop your own opinion about what's important. Yes, this is supposed to be a team exercise, but you are the leader and need to formulate your own vision to be sure the group time is well spent.

2. Once you've written a draft or sketched out your ideas, sit on them for a few days, weeks, or even months, and reference them while performing your day-to-day responsibilities. Do they make sense? Each time you have a decision to make, try to see how well it aligns with what you've written. Do you have enough freedom to be opportunistic while also staying within the framework you've established?

3. Get your core leadership team together and ask them to go through the same exercise.

4. Gather the team around a round table where you won't be disturbed; off-site is great. Define the day's objectives and have a plan for how you will step through the process.

5. Walk away from it all before making any commitments. Plan to come back to the work after taking the time to digest each statement. Look at what you've written and compare it to the mission and values statements of other great businesses known to depend on these documents. Start with

Johnson & Johnson, P&G, and any other companies that are similar to who you want to become.

6. Once you have a draft on paper, test it out. See how it feels. Look at the document, talk about it when making business decisions, bounce it off friends, family, even customers.

7. Make needed adjustments.

8. Commit to it. Print it. Own it. Share it with pride. Use it.

APPLYING THE MISSION AND VALUES STATEMENTS

Mission and values statements only have value, of course, if you apply them. You may have worked for a company whose tenets were never truly followed or adhered to — instead, they were just phrases on a wall or printing on the back of business cards. Ultimately, a lot of time and bandwidth were wasted creating something that will never be used.

Take the time to understand and implement mission and values statements with sincerity, so that they filter down into the veins and arteries of the business. To do this, you must resist the quarter-by-quarter mindset and year-by-year management style that focuses on short-term deliverables. You also must battle the emerging reality of the business world whereby people move around and change jobs so often that companies, especially larger ones, have an issue with continuity of thought. All of these conditions undermine the ability to plan for the long term, which is where mission and values statements excel as keepers of the core.

I made it my personal mission to ingrain these ideas into current and future employees. I talked about them constantly. We reviewed them at year-end performance discussions and brought them up at summer outings. I started team meetings highlighting one line selected from the mission and one from the values as a way to draw attention to a situation we had recently confronted. For example, when we had a customer communication issue, I highlighted "Communicate above expectations" and explained what that meant to me and to our organization. We discussed it as a team and tried to learn from our mistakes. When it was clear that people had been working harder than normal, I pointed out the importance of "To offer employees an attractive lifestyle opportunity" at a company-wide pizza party or barbecue.

I did everything I could to tie each moment of our collective professional experience to these pages that were hung on the walls in conference rooms and included in any presentation we made. This allowed these concepts to really become embedded in the organization. These ten (eventually eleven) lines of text became the constitution of the business, the shelter for our existence, and the defense against over-diversification. They became the simplified focus and the embodiment of our One Thing.

A company that expects greatness will invest the time and effort into sincerely pursuing the concept of mission and values statements. Remember, the mission and values statements are your core identity that forms the basis for the shell after shell you will grow into as your business prospers in the long future ahead. The mission and values statements are the tools to focus you on your One Thing and define where you are going. *Unless you know where you want to go, you'll never get there.*

- **Saying "no" may be more important than saying yes.**
- **Wasting time is a waste of time.**
- **Unless you know where you want to go, you'll never get there.**

CHAPTER THREE

THINK BIGGER

In the lobster community, hierarchies develop as the larger, stronger animals secure the best shelters, win the head-to-head physical battles, and assume dominant positions of superiority in the neighborhood. In business terms, we can imagine these creatures as the market leaders. When you're in business, you are essentially seeking to be the champion of your industry. In the process, you assume responsibility for strengthening the total market and protecting the industry. As the top lobster in the neighborhood, you grow and thrive in your community. In business, achieving scale comes from behaving as the biggest player in your space, even if you're not ... yet. Acting like you are shows that you expect to be in that role one day.

Today, four- and five-pound lobsters roam the ocean floors and by law are protected from being harvested because of their magnificent size. This protection increases their ability to propagate and grow the total lobster population. And while they didn't start out as the strongest creatures with the hardest shells, I have a feeling that these leaders of the community did have the attitude and personality necessary to achieve their size and strength — even before they molted successively. My premise is that if we want to be the leader of our industry and our community, we need to assume that posture from the beginning — regardless of our size when we start. We need to think like a leader and welcome opportunities that will grow our market potential.

When I joined Urnex, we were vulnerable. While we always managed to remain stable, during a six-month period at least ten of the top thirty customers abandoned our core products when a new competitor offered comparable products at lower prices. In reflection, I believe the challenges that come with over-diversification caused the loss of these customers to go unnoticed.

To help figure out what was happening, I took a leave of absence from the cushy security of my role at Unilever. Effectively, I did this by resigning while leaving every possible option available for a future return. I had not yet adopted the philosophy of "never leaving yourself an out." I was scared and uncertain of what I was getting into with the family business, and I was trying to hold onto the option of returning to the security offered by corporate America. Urnex was not behaving as a dominant leader. In the beginning, neither was I. It would take me a solid year to make the commitment to focus properly, get dedicated to One Thing, and expect success.

I read books to help me in my entrepreneurial pursuits, and if you're reading this, I assume you seek to become a leader in your industry (or at least be secure and protected from overfishing!). My tour around the United States to meet with each of the ten lost customers to learn what we'd missed and beg a second chance was the first of many lessons in humility. *Asking for a second chance is making a big commitment to never ask for a third.* Begging a customer to return is an experience we should all endure as it teaches the vulnerable feeling of needing someone else's support.

Eventually, we regained a business relationship with all ten of the key accounts through a diligent commitment to proving to each of those customers that ours was a business worth working with. Out of that experience, I developed a mindset of presenting the business at the scale, prestige, and level of professionalism that would make it worthy of the expectations of all customers.

My approach was that if you don't act like a big company, you will never become one. Before we get too much further, I want to make an important distinction: I am not recommending exaggerating your scale or your size. I am simply suggesting that you run your business, from day one, like the business you aspire to be well into the future, after the year-upon-year successive growth you expect and work toward.

From the beginning — whether I was meeting with customers who had dropped us or those who were loyal — my aspiration was to present the business to the outside world as the bigger organization that we aspired to be but had not yet become. Think about this for a second: How do you present yourself to the world? Act bigger, and bigger you will become (I imagine Yoda from *Star Wars* would say something like this).

Soon after an adult lobster molts, its new shell is bigger than the inner body. In fact, that fresh new shell is a full 10 to 15 percent larger than what's really inside. In terms of a business, there are many ways to show the world your bigger self as you take the time to grow. In the material that follows, you may find the modes of execution to be different for your business, but you'll also find overlap in the theory and accompanying strategies.

Take the mission and values statements from the preceding chapter; small, start-up businesses don't always incorporate such documents into the complicated process of getting going. Some never get around to defining things. I contend that those that skip these early steps will never grow to be extraordinary. They might make some money, have some fun, and gain some fame, but eventually, they will stall due to the lack of a plan.

These concepts are parts of the business that allow you to present yourself and your organization to the scale and standard you aspire to reach. Mission and values statements that are embedded in the organization have both operational and marketing value. They not only serve to focus and define your team's priorities, but can also impress customers and vendors (as well as competitors — we'll get to them later!) when you let them know you operate with such documents in place. In addition, just having these documents and articulating their value can attract top talent who want to work in a business that operates at this level.

By taking the time to craft thoughtful and meaningful mission and values statements, you are approaching your business with an expectation of greatness. Communicating this serves to present the business more favorably. As you'll see, it is all interconnected during this early larval stage of the business. We are building a framework (call it a shell) upon which to hang a larger entity in the future.

On the following pages, you will find examples of steps taken to enhance and expand the public persona of Urnex. While my experiences may not translate precisely to your opportunities, the intent is to give you ideas to consider and get you thinking of ways you can move your business forward and develop a shell into which you will grow. If you're still in the early stage of forming and shaping your business, recognize that each step you take when you are small and nimble can pay huge dividends as you grow. Eventually, you will appreciate and utilize the capacity you have built.

TECHNOLOGY/ERP:

Technological advances move fast ... and are getting even faster. When assessing your systems and upgrading where necessary, plan and invest for the future you dream of achieving. Don't limit your possibilities. You know molts are coming but you need the capacity to get through them.

For Urnex, one of our first, simple steps was to eliminate the "juno.com" email address the company was using. This was the year 2000 and although the internet was still new, it was already embarrassing to use a free email domain for professional services rather than an address of our own. We quickly invested in the urnex.com URL and created individual email addresses to end @urnex.com. We used all the mechanics and structures that we saw at previous corporations like Unilever and Salomon Brothers. So, despite the fact that we were small, I resisted the suggestion that emails should be "firstname@company.com." Instead, we used the formal "firstname.lastname@company.com." I was expecting that one day we might have many Steves and Alexas working on our team. This seems minor, but these little things lead to significance.

In our case, it was also important to upgrade the phone system. When I started, messages were left on a cassette tape recording machine of no higher quality than the one I had at home at the time. A long-term employee named Jen, who did a little bit of everything around the office, had recorded the greeting. She was a lovely woman with a thick New York accent, but I hoped our message would project more professionalism to represent the business. We invested in a sophisticated phone system and hired a voiceover artist to record the script that would play in place of hold music. Each word and idea shared on the new recording was carefully conceived to allow those listening to learn something new about the business.

For once, I didn't mind putting someone on hold as I imagined it as a chance to let them hear details about the company we might otherwise not get to tell them. It was not unusual for a customer who had waited a few seconds for their call to be answered to ask about the new Cafiza Espresso Machine Cleaning product they'd heard about on the recording. At the time, only "big players" could afford a pre-recorded hold message, so by investing in such a system, we presented as a big player. In today's world where phones are less important than they were twenty years ago, you must think about the caliber of your website and other public-facing collateral.

In your industry, you may have to follow different conventions than mine in order to present as a professional. The key is to think about how big and strong you want the world to see you, and to invest in those areas. Don't skimp on the seemingly simple things. Innumerable companies are in the business of helping you professionalize your online presence at a reasonable cost, with a result that is just as high quality as what you could pay multiples more for in design cost. Be sure not to be foolish in the areas where you save money. *Buy and invest for the scale you expect to achieve.*

Perhaps the biggest single technological investment a company makes is the Enterprise Resource Planning (ERP) or software package for measuring sales, purchasing raw materials, training key employees, collecting income, and recording customer transactions. This is the all-inclusive software foundation upon which your business's events and transactions are recorded — think SAP, a well-known brand of business solutions software. Regardless of the type of business you are in, you need a comprehensive system to organize, measure, and record how you're doing.

Do not rely on Excel spreadsheets and online accounting packages for anything other than a foundation toward understanding what it is that a future ERP system needs to help you manage. Think about the long term and where you aspire to arrive. What type of system will you need when you get there? Do not sell yourself short by getting by with software used by mom and pops. If you want to stop being a mom and pop, invest in this key area early.

The first major process-oriented and waste-elimination strategy I initiated was to seek out a comprehensive ERP system. When I joined the business, we were using a homemade system created by a guy named Frank. He was a nice guy who knew quite a bit about computers, but he was one guy and he knew nothing about running a business. His custom software system was built on business management processes that had been made up from scratch by individuals who had not been trained in established conventions of operational management. Aside from being clumsy and trouble-filled, each new process consumed an enormous amount of human bandwidth to create. What's more, it was all dependent on Frank.

No matter how unique an idea or business model you might have, it is still a venture that creates and sells a product or service. This means that along the way, a million business tasks are involved that others have already perfected. Finding the resources developed by experts will help you avoid distractions that take your effort away from your One Thing.

Urnex did not need to create its own software. Recognizing the availability of many off-the-shelf software packages to do the tasks we needed, we decided to invest a large sum in one comprehensive ERP package. The cost just about equaled what the company had invested for the previous five years! Every vendor I met while seeking to buy a system thought I was being a crazy over-spender and should use something simpler. To them, buying and installing this package was like using a bazooka to hunt a mouse.

It may have appeared as overkill to select a software package that was probably a hundred times more sophisticated than what we needed at the time. While we were doing about $2 million in combined annual sales (across seven product lines — and yes, that still included tube tops and lemon wedge bags), I bought a system that could accommodate a business doing $200 million per year or more. Well, as of the completion of this book, Urnex Brands still operates with that exact same software package, seventeen years later, and most recently with an annual EBITDA of about 275 times what it was when the package was installed. We never had to go through that investment again.

It was a self-fulfilling prophecy that the business grew to be worthy of the ERP selected — we grew to fit the shell. How did it work? A sophisticated, off-the-shelf ERP package forced our organization to follow processes and procedures that others had determined were the best practices. In effect, the outside world provided guidance on things we needed to implement. We were so small that we had to find rules to follow, and buying a software package intended for a larger company made us look bigger than we were while also helping us to get bigger.

As a side note, when the business was later being "diligenced" by potential investors, the private equity teams reviewed our IT systems. One of the experts auditing our system praised us for still using the off-the-shelf version of the ERP software with little to no customization. Apparently, many companies decide they must personalize such ERP systems for their needs. They feel that their business is so unique that a software package used by tens of thousands of businesses can't work for them. I believe this is a mistake and that perhaps my own humility — driven by starting out having to beg the top ten customers who had abandoned us to return — led me to this focused commitment to using what was available without feeling entitled to customize things.

By believing that your business is so different and so special that you can't adapt to a proven software package, you are giving way to your ego. From the start, my feeling was that we were no different from other businesses and if the system worked for them, it should work for us. We didn't need to differentiate ourselves by our system. We simply needed good records that allowed us to measure our progress and interact with our customers as would a larger organization.

TRADE PRESENCE:

When it comes to trade events, a well-conceived strategy focuses not only on designing your brand (see Chapter Five), but also executing it with an eye to representing your organization as larger than it may currently be. Your industry may not have trade shows, but you are certain to have networking events, lecture series, and other congregations of customers, competitors, and peers where you can learn and interact. Every public appearance you or your employees make is a part of your identity. Consistent trade show graphics, appropriate business attire for the message you hope to send, and more professional sales materials can all display your passion and surround your presence with the aura of a larger entity.

I've never been a fan of spending a lot of money or resources on developing printed matter or sales collateral (and even less so in today's world of emailable PDFs and a digital presence), but at times the audience is just looking for something to pick up and hold. Develop one powerful and simple printed message — based on your One Thing — that appeals to a wide audience, conveys your brand, and does so with elegance and efficiency. If such a sales brochure is adaptable and adjustable, it can provide you with great usage over the years, requiring only updated or changed packaging images and comments. In this way, you can save the bandwidth you would otherwise dedicate to frequently changing your brochure design (I'd put this in the "waste of time" category) and use it for other value-creating efforts.

When it comes to business attire, a similar philosophy works well. The people in the specialty coffee industry, which is one of many segments that Urnex served, are not a formally dressed crowd. When the Urnex team showed up in dark suits and ties with small logo pins on the lapels of their suit jackets, it must have presented a strange image to the T-shirt clad, tattooed baristas of Seattle and Portland. We knew what we were about, however, and it presented a solidity that our customers came to trust, and provided simplicity to the question new employees asked about how to dress. If it's not your style to dress in a suit and tie, don't do it. However, I would suggest you think about how you want to dress in business settings and communicate that to your organization. You have to feel comfortable and own the appearance. With that said, I don't think you can ever be overdressed at a professional event where you have the chance to meet existing and potential new customers. I maintain that this is a solid foundation for how a business presents to the world.

OFFICE SPACE:

Early on in my tenure at Urnex, I realized I had a problem with the physical appearance and comfort of the office space. At the time, we were based in Yonkers, New York. Just the name "Yonkers" made it tough to recruit as the town's reputation was one of faltering schools, governmental misconduct, and few attractive

places to go out for lunch or dinner. When a potential hire saw our more than modest offices, it was a tough sell. And so another major step in our growth was investing in upgrading our offices.

We spent a lot of money on thoughtfully selecting cubicle walls, dividers, carpet, and paint — considerably more than had been spent on the office space in the previous sixty-five years. I wanted to build a space where team members could work efficiently and that conveyed the seriousness of the business. This was another way of Thinking Bigger, designing an office that was an advertisement for the future — a space that said: Here, we are getting things done at the highest level of professionalism.

Prior to this investment in our space, we had a hard time attracting talent; it was difficult to recruit people to work at a coffee machine cleaning products company no one had heard of. So, we built an office for the scale of the company we expected to achieve ... and wouldn't you know, we quickly outgrew it. Later in the business's growth and expansion, we moved to a facility that was three times the one we'd been using for the previous ten years, and just five years later, took over adjacent space that had us in a facility ten times larger than the one where I started. The new space, worthy of the size we hoped to attain, triggered the most explosive improvements yet. We finally had room to expand and hire more and faster and better. You have to project yourself to where and what you expect to be in order to get there. *Without a target, you have no way to hit the bullseye.*

OUTWARD-FACING COMMUNICATION:

Presenting yourself as the company you want to be is the first step in becoming that company. Someone is always bigger than you are. You are not going to impress people with your sales numbers as much as you might impress them with other thoughtful ideas and bits of information. When customers asked me for our annual revenues, I just explained that we were a private company and we kept this information confidential. I left it at that and continued to build the image and concept and reputation that we were an organization of significance on any scale. As long as we presented and performed and delivered like people perceived the business, they trusted us and considered us to be a partner worth selecting.

I did share the number of employees on our payroll, the size of our facility, and as we grew, the number of countries in which we did business or where we had logistics centers (when those opened in Holland and Hong Kong). I'd advise you to look for ways to define your importance to the industry and your credibility within the market without having to share information that allows a competitor to learn more about you than you would like, or a customer to judge their importance (and use it to hurt you). For example, I never wanted our largest customer to know they were the largest. I found ways to explain that they were "top ten" but also quickly explained that we didn't have any customers that represented more than 10 percent of our sales (which was true). I always tried to protect the business from the vulnerability created by information oversharing. Sometimes, the ego gets in the way and then there is a risk of saying too much — at the expense of the long-term success of the business.

In effect, you want to be the biggest lobster in your space. Why would someone work with another company when you do your best to provide solutions, be responsive, and always protect them from missteps or points of vulnerability? Of course, it helps for people to know you have and use the tenets of mission and values statements, that you use a sophisticated ERP, and to see you dressed professionally.

Always remember, too, that your competitors are watching.

When it comes to the dominant player in the lobster community, smaller lobsters with aspirations are waiting for the moment when the dominant leader has to molt — that is an opportunity to take his place. I never wanted competitors to know when we were molting. The privacy of how we presented ourselves was a defense mechanism to ward off encroachment while also giving us flexibility on how we shared our story based on the audience.

Everyone you interact with is an audience to market to. This includes not only customers and competitors, but also vendors and employees. You want everyone to believe you are the professional organization that they expect. You communicate this professionalism by your responsiveness, your thoughtfulness, and your humility — it is real. By presenting your company to its internal and external audiences as the entity you aspire to be, you are living a self-fulfilling prophecy. Reflecting professionalism in documentation and reporting, marketing materials, email domains, phone numbers, and invoice design ensures that your current size doesn't matter so much as the size you imagine you will become.

- **Asking for a second chance is making a big commitment to never ask for a third.**
- **Buy and invest for the scale you expect to achieve.**
- **Without a target, you have no way to hit the bullseye.**

CHAPTER FOUR

KNOW YOUR AUDIENCE PART I: CUSTOMERS

Let's face it: it's a bit of a stretch to tell you that lobsters are deeply aware of their audience and surroundings in the way you need to understand your audience. While they do have amazing senses and are able to locate food and avoid danger through special antennules, lobsters are still relatively primitive creatures. Professor Michael Tlusty of the University of Massachusetts notes about lobsters: "They go out at night. They know their neighborhood … Lobsters are attuned to their environments." Sure, they get it, but they also get caught in the same traps over and over without learning that it's not a good idea to go into a cage for what seems like an easy snack. We need to be better than that. When it comes to how we know our audience and learn about a target consumer in business, we must be keenly perceptive and work to internalize and digest every aspect of our customer's profile and preference.

One of the most desperately important concepts in business success is the ability to separate our own wants and desires from those of our target audience and consumer. We must work hard to understand our audience so that we can gain their trust but also to deliver confidence, seal the deal, make the hire, or close the transaction. Perceptiveness and awareness of our audience and ourselves is the foundation of business success. *You are not your target audience.*

Any time you find yourself liking your own ad, appreciating your own new tagline, or speaking of your newest product as something you want to buy, stop yourself. Take a breath and remember that you have to remove yourself from the equation and understand your audience. It's not about what you like or desire. It's about your customer and his or her priorities. You know too much to rely on your own desires.

CONSUMER BEHAVIOR

I often tell those heading off to business school to be sure they take a course on Consumer Behavior. The course I took on this subject with Professor Sidney Levy at the Kellogg School was probably the foundation of everything I know about "knowing your audience." In that course, I learned to separate myself and my own interests and desires from those of the consumer target. I knew I had pulled it off when, early in my career in consumer product marketing, I considered taking jobs marketing feminine hygiene products and women's facial creams! I had never purchased or used any of the products I would be marketing, but I understood that the job of a marketer is distinctly separate from the marketer's own wants, desires, and preferences.

Thanks to Professor Levy, I entered the workforce understanding that if I made a business decision based on what "I liked" or what "I preferred" or what "I knew," I was probably making a mistake and failing to do my job as a marketer or manager. As a side note, I consider marketing part of and the core essence of management. As managers, we are marketing to all those inside and out of the organization, and the fundamental premise of marketing is to know your target consumer. Sometimes, our consumer is a person we manage on our team.

In this book, I won't redefine the academic discipline of Consumer Behavior, a time-honored focus on recognizing who is in your audience: their age range, gender, household income, zip code, family dynamic, etc. That is classical consumer marketing that I'm in no way suggesting you abandon. The core of the process goes like this: *our target customer is a woman, a mother with an average of 2.3 children all under the age of 12, living in a suburban community defined by zip code with a household income of >$75,000. She may have 2 cars and be in the age range of 35 to 49.*

That textbook stuff is great. It is essential to the analytical portion of your mission to delight a specific customer by defining him or her objectively. But what's more exciting and more valuable is the psychographic definition of this consumer. First, what is psychographic? Oxford online defines it as: "The study and classification of people according to their attitudes, aspirations, and other psychological criteria, especially in market research."[iv] This is defining who they are, what they like, and how they feel about things.

With a small business, we did not do formal, quantitative market research. However, I don't think a day went by when we were not gathering and assessing the qualitative elements of our audience. What motivates them? What worries them? What excites them? Are they rushed all the time? Do they take joy in our product or simply see it as a necessity (or hassle)? By recognizing these needs in our audience and the psychological elements that shape their identity, we gain trust and a willingness to collaborate. You must interact with your customers and learn their tendencies and try to tailor your thinking to their interests.

Here's an easy example: I am not the target audience for this book today. By definition, I (hopefully!) already know everything it contains. However, I was a perfect candidate to read it fifteen years ago. In the process of writing this book, I had to realize that you are my audience. I recognize that it is my job to think about what is important to you and what value and insight and education I can offer you. You're reading this book because you're hoping to pull out a tidbit or two that will help you make your business more successful. You probably don't expect this to be the key to all your problems. You hope it's entertaining, relatable, and able to help you think through a problem from a new angle. I'm guessing that you will appreciate short chapters containing focused ideas so you can digest them in pieces as your busy schedule permits. Thinking like your customers and anticipating what is important to them gets easier as soon as you begin to separate yourself from them.

The previous chapters can stand us in good stead here because the concept of knowing your audience goes hand in hand with that of self-awareness. We start in business by understanding who we are and what our organization represents, where it excels and what needs to improve. In learning about our consumer and our target audience, we operate with humility about ourselves, which includes a realistic appraisal of what we're good at and what we offer that our target audience wants and appreciates. We then take that understanding and focus on building up our organization and positioning ourselves to the world in a way that will appeal to our audience.

I AM NOT A CONSUMER OF MY PRODUCTS

Why is this so important? Because I was not — and am still not to this day — the consumer of my products. That distinction might be easier to understand if you realize that I'm only slightly closer to being a consumer of coffee machine cleaner than I am to being a user of hair conditioner today (see bald picture on my website). Before I joined Urnex, I was not a particularly astute or regular coffee drinker and I don't think I had ever cleaned a coffee machine. Coffee is still not an essential part of my morning. I enjoy unusual coffees from unique origin countries, but I don't obsess over finding them as do many important Urnex customers. The lesson here is that you don't need to love or even like the things that are important to your business's audience to understand how they think. I didn't need to love coffee to do my job. I just needed to understand it enough to understand my audience. Over the years, I have had the pleasure of visiting coffee farms in El Salvador and Costa Rica where I harvested coffee cherries along with the local migrant workers. From these experiences, I have gained a fuller understanding of what is important to our customers and how passionate they are about coffee.

Thinking like your consumer is a hard lesson that I've observed many business owners struggle to learn. Continuing in the vein of my business as a proxy for yours, some of my hires were not coffee drinkers and thought this would make it more difficult for them to do their jobs. One person I hired, Ronald, decided that, because he didn't drink coffee, he didn't need to think about the coffee audience at all. However, after being dragged to coffee cupping after coffee cupping and eventually to Costa Rica to work on a coffee farm, Ronald came to me and explained his revelation: "This is a customer that's so different from me but knowing that allows me to understand what I need to do to make them happy with our products."

If you are not like your target audience, it doesn't have to be a detriment. In fact, it may help you look at your audience with fewer distractions if you open your mind to learning what is important to them. You can develop an ability to think like the consumer and understand their psychology. To do this, you must read what they read, immerse yourself in their environment, explore their priorities and problems, and in the case of Ronald, get to see their lives and what motivates them.

Dive right into your customer's exact life today. Try to think about what might have gotten them to this point. Regarding those who operated in the world of coffee, I asked myself: Was it a family business? Were they recovering from an earlier failure, and this industry offered a fresh start with a special appeal? Did they follow the inspiration of a spouse? Did a great teacher lead them to this career? Was it the need to pay for school that got them started? Maybe they don't even like the industry, but they have a good job and it lets them pursue other personal priorities.

In the next section, you will read about my immersion in the world of coffee. That is your cue to think about what experiences might be necessary for you regarding your business. You can engage with an industry in many ways. You might find a cooking course if you are in the food service industry, or a coding course if you sell software. The questions remain the same: Who are you talking to? What is important to them? What excites them, worries them, and outright scares them? Once you understand that your audience is not you, then you can begin to discover what is important to them and market to them with that newfound knowledge.

One last piece of advice and the "how to": You have to apply yourself to this effort. One trip to visit a few coffee shops or attending one barista event was not going to suffice for me to learn my audience. First, I needed to figure out how to learn it and then continue to engage with it in an ongoing way. We don't learn everything about a subject on the first pass. This goes with the concept of incrementalism; we must layer on our learning and internalize the importance of identifying with our audience. This is the job.

THE WORLD OF COFFEE

When I first decided to enter the world of coffee, I knew nothing about the industry or my audience. I had never visited Seattle, the capital of US coffee. At that point, my knowledge of the city was limited to a bad experience with the Seattle Mariners beating the New York Yankees in the 1995 playoffs, and what I saw in the film *Singles*. On my first trip to Seattle, I visited the hot spots of coffee at the time. I went to the original Starbucks store and the headquarters where I was able to meet with a buyer for the one product they had been using ever since their first store opened the year I was born. I tried coffees (something I rarely consumed previously) from Peet's, Tully's, Seattle's Best, and then found my way into Pegasus.

I still remember the epiphany of great coffee for the first time at Pegasus Coffee. It was a taste and a warmth and a luxury I had not previously understood. I sat quietly and enjoyed it. I had a fast-paced, investment-banking-trained New York mindset, and I didn't know what to do or what it meant to sit in a café and drink a coffee. I was confused but as I tasted this coffee, I understood. There was something special to this beverage that was unlike anything I had ever experienced, and from there I had an epiphany about why the industry I was about to enter had something special in the works.

During this trip, I started to "feel" Seattle. I slept in modest hotels, hung out in coffee shops, ate at the market stalls, observed the baristas interacting with their customers, and found time to hike in the Hoh Rain Forest on my way to Vancouver and Victoria, BC, in Canada, where I continued my discovery trip. I was on a mission to understand the audience and see what life was like for them.

In college, I had been exposed to the music of Nirvana by the guy who lived next door to me on my hall, and I became a fan. Like many, I was saddened when Kurt Cobain left us. As part of that trip, I made my way to Aberdeen, Washington, to see where Cobain was from and where Nirvana began. Somehow, I found a connection between grunge music and the cold, dampness of the air in this coastal town with high unemployment and frequent rain. I saw the incomparable somberness leading to the angst that I heard in the music. I felt aware of my audience and started to connect these influences to my understanding of the coffee community. I knew it was a generalization, but I was looking for a link between myself and this part of the country. Somehow, this cold, wet, dark area helped me start to understand why coffee made sense to many people and why the Pacific Northwest was an obvious place for a lot of coffee to be consumed.

Soon after I returned from my tour of the Pacific Northwest, I set up a makeshift espresso station in my office and spent time using David Schomer's book *Espresso Coffee: Professional Techniques* to teach myself how to be a barista. At that time, Schomer was a sort of an eccentric godfather of specialty coffee, teaching people how to make coffee Seattle-style while wearing his signature bolo ties. I had just been to his coffee shop, Vivace, on my tour, and I was amazed by the attention to detail of his baristas. David was revered as a near-deity who inspired people to leave their jobs and start coffee shops following his tenets of quality and purity in the cup. I got pretty good at calibrating my grinder, understanding the right pressure to use when tamping the coffee, and eventually pulled off some decent latte art. Most important in all of this was that I worked hard to experience the day-to-day activities of my audience.

Even though making coffee has historically been the job of corporate underlings and assistants, the specialty coffee baristas found a way to valiantly elevate the job out of that stereotype. I wanted to feel and touch the machine and the ground coffee and see the mess it creates in my mission to know the customer. This is the reason everyone at the Starbucks corporate headquarters once trained to be a barista. It's also the reason I made many on my staff learn to make their own espresso and cappuccino, brew filter coffee, and of course, clean all the machines.

What I found to be special about immersion in the profession was seeing the passion and the pursuit of this sort of coffee nectar that the barista purists aspire to infuse into each espresso. The effort and repetition showed me my audience. I learned they were a like-minded community dedicated to a special product. These are people who work incredibly hard to build their own expertise, to help support the coffee farmers who grow their products, and to collaborate as if each is a family organization. This audience wants honesty and quality. They want to be able to relate to their suppliers and they want to know that their ideas and thoughts are respected and understood. In order to serve that community and become their cleaning product of choice, we needed to understand and respond to all the ways that they thought, and recognize what was important to them.

THIS IS PROBABLY TRUE IN ANY INDUSTRY

In every industry, there are people who get excited about the things they do each day. While I was learning that coffee is a passionate industry and a place for people to build both a career and an identity, I'm sure your industry includes a point of view that you can engage with to understand how to optimally do your job. This isn't a sales trip. This is a market research project where you want to learn your audience experientially.

I imagine that if I were in the seafood industry, I'd go fishing or spend time in a canning factory. If I were in the meat industry, I'd want to know cattle farmers and butchers. In aerospace, I'd probably visit all I could related to NASA, rocket launches, and hands-on space camp experiences in an attempt to understand my audience. And so on. Throughout my career, I have looked at what's happening in other industries and compared the personalities and attitudes of specialists in other businesses with mine. While coffee is special to me, the same lessons and rules about people apply in other places. Coffee is not alone in its dedication and passion as a community.

For example, the independent pet store industry (not Petco or the big box stores) represents about 50 percent of the pet supply market.[v] Much like independent bookstores in the *You've Got Mail* era, this industry is filled with passionate experts who know and love what they do. Many are in business not because they aspire to make enough money to retire early, but because they love animals and pets — just like coffee roasters and baristas love coffee and the experience it provides. You can find similar groups and profiles in the craft beer industry, hardware, art, hair/make-up, cabinet making, technology, gaming, and many other spaces. These owners and entrepreneurs have an appreciation for great products. They think about what is important to them, and that effort allows them to make choices based on brand identity, values, and efficacy.

At Urnex, we had a passionate and meticulous audience that was and is willing to pay a little more for the best. In an industry dominated by passion and dedication, this is the opportunity to create value rather than solely compete with commodities. The premium you seek to command is the direct link to the kind of growth this book hopes to help you achieve.

KNOWING YOUR CUSTOMER ALSO HELPS YOU TO INNOVATE

Knowing your audience not only allows you to deliver existing products and services efficiently and effectively — it also allows you to innovate much more seamlessly. A great example of when knowing your audience led to an opportunity to satisfy a huge customer was my experience launching an ice machine cleaning product for coffee shops. While ice machines may seem like a potential deviation from our One Thing, I felt very confident that this was not an unfocused distraction. As we reflected on our mission and values statements, we determined that ice machines were an integral part of the coffee community, as iced coffee was a huge part of the business. Helping maintain the ice preparation equipment was in line with our mission: *To make and sell products that fill specialty market needs.* Ice machine cleaner was surely a fit.

One afternoon, I received a phone call from Vivian, the head of quality and hygiene at Starbucks. She called a bit panicked after realizing the newly implemented corporate safety policy (which I imagined she had something to do with developing) would ban one of their existing cleaning products from their stores. The new policy stated that if any products with a pH (acid/basic scale) level of below 2.0 were used, then the store would need to install an expensive emergency eyewash station on-site. Apparently, the ice machine cleaner they had been using for years had a pH below 2.0.

When the call came, Vivian explained the situation and then asked: "Do you have an Ice Machine Cleaner with a pH above 2.0?" My answer, as you might expect, was based on my awareness of the stress level in her voice and my imagination that she might have approved this new policy without knowing that the ice machine cleaner currently in distribution was in conflict:

"Why yes, of course, let me get you some samples. I'm not sure we are in stock so it might take a couple of days to get it out to you, but we should be able to have it very quickly."

Now, if you know a little bit about me by now you might guess that we had no such product. However, I was quick to answer "yes" with confidence as I was representing the brand as who we aspired to be and who I knew we could be. As an organization, we had talked about making an ice machine cleaner, but we didn't have it yet. What I did in that situation was to assess my audience, imagine the problem she was experiencing, and provide a solution to what I knew she wanted. Of course, I was more than happy to provide another product to this then-nearly 20,000-store chain.

Step one was researching and testing the competitive product in use as well as all the others on the market. We had to know everything we could. Step two was finding ice machines to clean. I remembered that an accountant who had worked on our tax returns mentioned that her husband ran operations for a group of Marriott Hotels in New Jersey. Following on the concept of immersion, I was able to get myself invited for a day of the regularly scheduled ice machine cleaning at a Marriott near Trenton, New Jersey, to further learn the audience and hence the industry.

I was embedded with the maintenance staff who explained that ice machines were cleaned monthly. Corporate inspection started with a visual review of the clarity of ice on each floor of a hotel. Cloudy ice cubes indicate a failure to clean and represent a hygiene risk. So, after a day of cleaning ice machines and testing the prototypes we had made, I understood what was involved, figured out how to write easy-to-follow usage instructions, and sent Vivian a sample of Freez Ice Machine Cleaner.

The rest is history. The point here is that in order to understand the product and the audience, I had to have spent a lot of time understanding the customer and knowing her well enough to sense the tension in her voice. On top of that, developing the product required us to live it and work with the equipment and think like the customer we aspired to serve. I don't know if Vivian was, in fact, partly responsible for the new pH policy and potential eyewash stations, but I'd bet she had something to do with it. My knowledge of her personality and the industry allowed me to respond in a way that she appreciated. So often we have opportunities to take awareness of what makes a client tick, and turn it into a growth potential that also helps the client. I had worked hard to think like my audience, understand her psychographic profile, and react in a manner that she appreciated deeply. All this served to enhance the Urnex brand.

Once you've got it in your mind that what you think or what is important to you doesn't matter as much as what your audience wants, you are equipped to build a business for consistent and controlled growth. You have given yourself the tools to impress and delight your audience by your awareness of their psychology and priorities. Putting on the hat of your target and identifying their mindset allows you to efficiently create ideas and responses and suggestions that will appeal to them. It's all about knowing who you're talking to, what motivates them, and internalizing that information so you can respond, satisfy, and inspire them.

(• **You are not your target audience.**

CHAPTER FIVE

CREATE A POWERFUL BRAND

A powerful brand image can be likened to a lobster's shell. Think of the beautiful red shell of a steamed lobster and your mind probably goes to summer holidays, fine dining, and the pleasures of time by the seaside. A strong brand — the company's public persona — stands out as the framework for all the worldly interactions of your business. All of the work you have put into discerning your One Thing, crafting mission and values statements, and learning your audience, can now be expressed through a brand so that your customers, vendors, and competitors both know and feel exactly what you stand for.

A lobster's shell provides not only protection but also stability through the strength of its structure, which supports what is inside. Even as your business grows and matures, a strong brand remains a constant and consistent part of your business identity. Each time a lobster molts, the outer shell hardens around the core more rigidly than each previous iteration. In a similar way, your brand identity may adapt to new situations and evolve slightly as part of your marketing campaigns, but if conceived properly and supported with deep conviction and attention to detail, it doesn't need to change dramatically. It is the same foundational part of your identity.

Early on, if you can commit to your brand and what it stands for, everything you do and every action you take serves as reinforcement. Contemplating a decision about what is best for the business will often involve asking yourself if an action is best for the brand. Through the actions you take and the images you present to your audience, you accumulate a currency of protective strength we call brand equity. Much like the shell of a lobster, this is your security and the value you are creating (see *Chapter Fourteen: An Exit of Scale*).

THE BRAND SPEAKS INSIDE AND OUT

As with the lobster's shell, the brand does not only face outward. Those on the inside of the business must internalize the brand just as they must take to heart the mission and values statements, and work to know the audience. Creating this inner corporate (corporeal) framework upon which all your other public personas and interactions are based and built is the first step to really owning it. When thinking about hiring, for example, who do you want to represent the brand? How do they sound when they speak to someone on the phone? What is their attitude like? How do they treat the customer? Are their care, intelligence, and professionalism apparent in their articulations and appearance? For my customer service focused model, I wanted everyone to have that humbled sense of self-worth because that is what the brand stands for. If you remember in Chapter Three, I also believe that the way you and your team dress and present serves both to build the image and the brand of the business. Everything is interconnected.

Your brand starts with the story you tell by your actions: the confidence you command from your team and your customers and suppliers, and the essence of what you stand for. It is what you have articulated through the mission and values statements and the expression and understanding of your target audience and your One Thing. But it doesn't end there. Your brand is represented by your follow-through and reliability, and by the commitments you make.

When Urnex clients asked for products or services, we were honest about whether or not we could deliver them. While at times, I promised things before I was certain exactly how delivery would occur (like ice machine cleaner), once I made a promise on behalf of the brand, all necessary bandwidth was applied to delivery. Our brand was about commitments fulfilled without exception. We always figured out how to support the brand because failure to do so meant betraying the standards we had established.

Every day that you are out there representing a brand to the public, you must take responsibility and commit yourself to follow-through. Showing your long-term commitment to honesty, credibility, and reliability — and not short-term gain — is how you build a trusted brand. For me, the brand became an expression of all the people assembled together to support the business.

Growing, strengthening, and hardening your brand means thinking for the future and holding the core meaning of that brand as an unwavering commitment. When you've done this for a while, you build up trust in the brand and that trust will be there to help get you through any difficult time when your shell has molted and you are vulnerable. I had more than one of these moments of vulnerability (see Chapter Twelve). But even apart from a crisis, the process of developing and defining your brand is one of the single most important actions and efforts you can take in positioning your business for controlled, disciplined, and consistent growth.

A brand that embodies the product, the company, and the team of managers will command a premium price for its products in the market, and this is the key to business profitability. Remember — like in business — for great success, the brand has to stand on its own and be bigger than any smaller part.

Nearly every service that you provide is likely available somewhere else. Most products are or will eventually become commodities (iPods, mp3 players, cornflakes, televisions). However, those businesses that present and develop a brand identity that differentiates their products from those of similar offerings of competitors are the ones that survive and thrive. What is ownable about your brand? What is the equity in your brand? The equity in your brand is what a future acquirer will appreciate. The lack of brand equity was a reason I exited the tube top and lemon cover businesses. You can get soap or rice or motor oil anywhere, but you pay more for Dove or Uncle Ben's or Pennzoil. It feels safer to buy the brand. It offers accountability and confidence not available from commodities.

EXTERNAL PRESENTATION OF THE BRAND

Your brand is the foundation of the business it supports. You need intense focus and dedication to build a brand for growth. I hope you understand that a strong brand permeates your organization and commands alignment both internally and externally. Now, I'm going to get a little more tactical and share the executional elements of a brand. While each one is important, remember that the tactic, design, media placement, or advertisement you develop is wasted without a brand that speaks and presents tenets to which the organization has dedication and conviction.

When you sell things that have value and for which your

customers want to pay a premium, you earn your return by delivering on your promise and convincing your customers that it is worth buying from you. So how do you convince them? Use the following four elements to express a brand that is aligned with your company's core philosophy. These four concepts are not intended to replace the "4Ps" of classical marketing. [vi] Later on, you can work through "product, price, placement, and promotion." Those are tactical. Before you can execute, you have to know who you are and define yourself and your brand. Just as you've found your One Thing, focused on it, and identified your mission and values ... you now have to share it with the world. Let's go through your logo, communication and collateral, packaging, and taglines.

LOGO

Part of your brand is, of course, your logo. While a consistent, distinctive, clear, and visually powerful logo is essential, the logo isn't all there is to the brand. In fact, the logo is merely a mnemonic for how you summarize and present all the other foundational decisions you've made to focus the business. It is the tool you use to grant impressions of your brand to the world, and it is the image of your brand people retain.

When people are asked to name the best logos in the world, they usually pick those of companies like Coke, Apple, Nike, and Google. I'd argue that people praise these logos as graphically brilliant not because they have excellent designs, but rather because the products and outward identities of the companies they represent are already world-class. Which comes first? To me, it is obvious: build a great company and it will be forever remembered regardless of its logo design. Of course, adding a great logo to the equation can further enhance your identity and inspire customers and employees. At the same time, remember that an unreliable company offering mediocre products is unlikely to become great because of a beautifully designed logo.

Since a logo is a representation or shorthand for the brand, the look and feel must communicate your mindset and the values of your brand. It should be memorable and it should stand alone. Also, think about how it looks when you set it beside other logos (check the angles with a ruler if you want to be really intense). Does it carry the right gravitas? How does it work in black and white? Are the words and letters difficult to read? Do you need so many letters? Remember that keeping it simple means that the same logo can work across multiple size executions. These are things we don't always think about.

The logo I started with was the same small oval shaped somewhat like a target that had been in existence since the 1940s. It worked and it already had some brand equity. However, the company lacked discipline in consistently using the same logo in all executions. I set out to impose a brand standard and eliminate variations so that every impression of the logo was consistent. Before that time, some versions of the brand were shown with a shadow drop, others used a monotone, and still others were inconsistent in the colors. We streamlined and defined how our logo should work and started using one logo with consistency and frequency — and focus. The most important recurring theme in brand work is to define the details up front, or as soon as they present themselves, so that you don't have to consume valuable bandwidth rethinking things. We defined our Pantone colors, consolidated variations of the logo used throughout time to one structure, and stuck to it. The lesson here is the same as in your mission and values statements: it's important to be consistent.

If you already have a logo, I'm not espousing changing it. In fact, like me, you have a huge opportunity to reinforce that logo by finding ways to consolidate its power and simplifying it to make sure it is used consistently. If you are just starting out, you will probably go to a design firm or use one of many great online professional services options for help. Just remember that your logo doesn't need to appeal to you as its primary audience. It needs to speak to your audience. It has to keep them in mind and be deeply consistent, easy to read, and recognizable across many mediums such as print, online, billboards, and sales collateral.

COMMUNICATIONS AND COLLATERAL

Communicate with your customers individually or in groups using a variety of techniques. First, work hard to find the right cadence of delivery of phone calls, emails, and newsletters. More than that, you need the right content. You need content that your audience will appreciate that offers value for the time they spend consuming it. As you develop content and find the right pace for its delivery, it makes sense to start out conservatively. When people appreciate and thank you for your levels of contact, you know you are onto something. When they don't mention it, joke about the barrage, or just unsubscribe, you know you're off base.

Many automated systems can maintain and build contacts. I preferred sending loads of personal emails and making hundreds of phone calls. During my tenure running Urnex, it was not uncommon for people to come up to me at a trade event, say hello, and introduce me to their colleagues as the "Hello from Urnex guy."

In my effort to keep in touch with contacts and connections, I sent many emails using the subject line "Hello from Urnex." These emails were a few sentences of regards, thanks for their consideration of some specific item, or a request for follow-up on one thing or another discussed previously. They were short, focused, and sent at intervals that seemed appropriate for each contact. In addition, I used that simple, recurring subject line because it had the potential to become memorable after repeated exposure.

It all comes down to the fine line between frequency and redundancy, between *showing* your brand constantly without appearing *showy*. Many businesses have this internal debate about the value of advertising. Much has changed from the days of print media's dominance to the digital world of today, but I believe the same principles can be applied to any situation.

Prior to my joining, Urnex had been playfully creative in changing advertising executions every few months or from periodical to periodical. My experiences at Unilever were similar in that the brand and advertising teams regularly changed creative executions to keep the campaign exciting. The mindset was that we owed it to our audience to entertain them with new messages and to keep things fresh. However, I didn't think many people paid attention to our ads until they had seen them three, four, five or more times.

To me, all the effort going into each execution was distracting resources from other things. Running a small business with a limited budget meant we had little extra time to make decisions about advertising every week, month, or quarter. You probably don't either. If you are constantly reworking advertisements, consider asking yourself what else you could do with that time and/or money? Is the incremental return from a constantly refreshed advertising campaign worth the drain of the resources required to make it excellent?

Since the human mind has a hard time remembering things, I wanted our message to be seen everywhere with repetitive consistency. Given our limited resources, our team worked diligently to prepare one advertisement, with one logo and message, that would run in every magazine and web banner for the entire year or longer! The consumer would never retain a memory of any of those ads if they saw them once and never again. By running the same ad every time for long campaigns, it began to feel like the Urnex brand was ubiquitous. We stopped any need for an internal debate about the brand. We had reached team alignment and moved on to the next task at hand. This approach was right for our business. You'll have to reflect on this and see how it applies to yours.

PACKAGING

Product packaging, or, in the case of a service industry, presentation formats and files, must likewise consistently convey the value of the brand. Are you starting to see the pattern? Everything we do needs to conform to the brand identity. Through consistency, you convey confidence, professionalism, and clarity about your own identity to the outside world. Disorder, inconsistency, and lack of focus, on the other hand, lead customers, vendors, and employees to stray from the mission you have set for yourself and for which you seek their buy-in. Distraction and lack of order consume the bandwidth of your customers. You want them focused on what you are offering, not consumed by the need to interpret your package or design.

Many facets of the business can benefit from thoughtful packaging which does not present a drag upon your efficiency. Just as the same advertisement can run for years, you can gain a lot of benefit from setting up one brochure or package design that can be updated, having one consistent in-house font, and building an architecture for your physical packaging by which new products can easily expand off the existing line. It became important to me to use colors to differentiate products within the same family that offered similar benefits. You can think of it as a portfolio of hair care products with multiple formulas under one brand, where red is for thin hair, blue for thick, yellow for curly, etc. When you discover there is a market for people with a new type of hair, all you have to do is pick another color and you have your next product extension ready to go without distracting you or the team with the troublesome and time-consuming work of brand and packaging design. Here's a look at a packaging architecture change Urnex implemented during our "Mature Adult" phase after we had taken care of a lot of smaller projects and had time to tackle the bigger ones.

Before   After   vii

As you will notice, we started with a group of brands and packaging that had consistency only in the placement of our logo at top center (and even then, not perfectly consistent, as you see in the product that is third from left in the top photo). Each of our sub-brands had its own font and identity, which prevented us from presenting an organized, professional, customer-facing product lineup.

While these were all business-to-business brands you were unlikely to see on a retail shelf, we took a step forward in how we presented our brand, and this ultimately led to our customers expanding the numbers of SKUs they purchased from us as they saw a family and realized *the opportunity to enjoy high resale margins* on more items.

We tidied things up and sought to organize and define how the world saw us. More importantly, we achieved enormous cost savings by eliminating the need to stock four or five different color caps. By consolidating our purchasing to only white caps, our operating margins and warehouse utilization efficiencies increased dramatically. Thoughtful packaging and representation of our brand paid dividends across a wide spectrum. While it started out as a simple plan to graphically tighten up packaging design, the project led to great results. Do you have similar opportunities where making one improvement can lead to others?

TAGLINES AND TARGET AUDIENCES

Along with a logo, brand name, and overall positioning, tag lines form the underpinning of a business and align the team. A tagline can be used as a foundation that you come back to with every pivot point in the business. It's a gut check like your mission and values, but on a more near-term, product-specific time horizon. Taglines should also connect to the idea that a brand is both internal and external. The tagline is as important to bringing the sales and marketing team together behind a unified message as it is to conveying that message to the consumer. Throughout my time in the coffee cleaning products business, I refused to refer to Urnex as a maker of chemicals. I always positioned the company as one that made products that "helped the consumer make better tasting coffee." In knowing our target audience, I realized that they didn't like chemicals or the idea of chemicals, as I'd learned from my visits to the Pacific Northwest. Those who gravitated to coffee didn't want to think that anything possibly dangerous was coming near their beloved beverage. By talking about the way our products improved the taste of their product, we found a warmer way to connect. The goal of our tagline became to distinguish the essence of our brand from other commodity products for similar purposes. "Helping People Make Better Tasting Coffee" encapsulated the idea that no matter who you were or what your taste in coffee might be, our products and company were behind you to make your coffee better. It told the story of the brand. Your brand and your tagline should talk to the widest audience possible. Don't limit yourself by choosing the wrong words. Had we decided we were helping people make "perfect coffee," we probably would have eliminated about 95 percent of the potential customers in our market, just from our story. Most people in the coffee industry don't and can't aspire to make "perfect" coffee. They just want to make it better, as the goal with coffee is just to enjoy it. Here we found a way to express our brand by taking into account the breadth of our audience. How could this lesson apply to your business?

In the previous examples, you can start to see how Urnex became a brand business and the few key, simple rules to focus the presentation of the brand to its audience. We determined from day one that we would support and develop the brand as our highest priority. Many great chemists can make outstanding cleaning products. We didn't necessarily have better chemists or better formulas. However, we had focus and aspiration and self-awareness about what we wanted to be, and we had an aligned brand identity. Urnex Brand products were well-formulated with a deep understanding of the application and requirements of our audience in the coffee industry. However, they were still relatively simple and not that different from soap. As my friend Dave at Unilever used to say, "Soap all goes down the drain eventually." The Urnex Brand was not just about great products. It was about respect for the coffee industry and awareness of our audience. While the soap may go down the drain, the impression of the brand remains strong in the memory. *Without a brand, you are without an identity.*

Your brand is everything you present to the world both internally and externally. It is who you are as a market leader and it is your business's trusted reputation. It is also your inner conscience and, last but certainly not least — the hard shell and equity upon which your business is based.

) • **Without a brand, you are without an identity.**

PART TWO:
MATURE ADULT — FISHABLE BUT STABLE

PART TWO

In the first few chapters, we talked about the foundational investments for the future that we need to make in our business while we are fresh and nimble. As a lobster grows and matures to the legal minimum size eligible for harvest, the molt process slows to a pace of about once per year. With each molt, a more dramatic evolution of the lobster occurs, as growing 15 percent represents a much larger absolute increase in size and a much more challenging molt process.[3]

During Part Two or the Mature Adult phase of a business, we are now more concerned with our larger internal team of employees, their alignment, and the way information is shared across the organization. We must start thinking about our customers, employees, and competitors with a different kind of intimacy as our new scale and invested capital make us more dependent on keeping them and growing with them.

For Urnex, this phase meant that we needed to focus on avoiding waste, documenting our priorities, managing our cash flow, and presenting ourselves to the world with consistency. The business had matured and we were an adult. We were running a viable entity upon which many employees and their families depended, and our contributions to the economy were significant. At this stage in a business's maturity, you can no longer go unnoticed.

What was most interesting and exciting was that the business had reached a maturity where — if we'd done our job well — each 15 percent growth of topline sales could generate

---

3 An annual goal of 15 percent topline growth every year was right for our starting size of less than $1 million of sales in the category where we were focused. Growing a certain percent means different things to different size businesses. Growth of 15 percent per year is easier to achieve when a company is smaller, despite the fact that a larger organization has more resources at hand. In absolute revenue, a business of $100,000 growing $15,000 per year is a different proposition than one of $100,000,000 growing $15,000,000, in terms of the number of salespeople, invoices to process, and so much more.

significantly more profits. We had laid a foundation and could put on that next 15 percent of topline growth with operational efficiency as we grew into the capacity we built in earlier years. We no longer needed to add a person to take responsibility for every new account or production operation, as our existing team was more than capable of managing a few more clients and our production lines and ERP system were ready to be fully utilized.

Under the laws of the State of Maine: "A legal lobster is harvestable when it ... has a carapace or body shell length that measures between 3 ¼ inches and 5 inches."[viii] Translating this into years, it means that a lobster really only has a three- to four-year window during which it can be fished. It is during the critical, fishable time in the life of a lobster that self-preservation and awareness are all important. This period of vulnerable maturity feels a lot like the middle years of my Urnex journey. The ancillary product lines had been shed, the coffee machine cleaning business was established as our One Thing, and we were now ready to set the stage to get to a new level. Before that could happen, however, we had more work to do.

In a three- to four-year window, the business had become mature and stable. We were growing consistently and making tough choices about where to dedicate resources. During this time, the business was professionalized from a proprietorship led by a few to an organization led by a team of many who were all following mutually agreed tenets and philosophies. We learned that not all employees could grow with the business, we focused efforts on waste reduction, we identified the true importance of thinking about the competition, and we developed a strategy for doing so. The foundations developed and the lessons learned in the early years were of obvious value as we entered the next phase.

CHAPTER SIX

KNOW YOUR AUDIENCE PART II: EMPLOYEES

In many ways, the concept of being aware of the priorities of those around us is just basic human courtesy. A line in the Simon and Garfunkel song "The Sound of Silence" is one that I like to share with my children when they are rushing through a conversation. It goes like this: "People hearing without listening."[ix]

We hear without listening all the time. We're so caught up in our own problems that we don't take the time to think about those with whom we're interacting. What's going on in their lives? Are your employees troubled by something at home? Are your kids worried about pleasing or disappointing you — or are they just fixated on a new app they want your approval to buy? Does your partner have a vision for himself or herself in the future that you can help them attain?

All of these groups of people are your audience. If you separate your own desires from those of your audience, you have an opportunity to be a better listener. There comes a time in the maturation of your business when you have the base in place and you are ready to build your dream team. Knowing your employees and figuring out how to get the most from them is a key part of moving from a business that is in an early stage to one that's more mature. It starts with good listening.

In Chapter Four, we talked about knowing our audience through the lens of the consumer and how we can translate the long process of immersion, self-analysis, and deep investigation into what motivates and inspires our clientele. But knowing your audience is a much broader concept than simply trying to understand the target buyer in the traditional marketing sense. The same lesson about working to separate our own priorities from those of our customers applies to the people who work with us. Each effort we make to think like those we work with allows us to use that knowledge to be a better collaborator, while at the same time, keeping the attainment of our goals a top priority.

When I graduated college and interviewers asked me what I wanted out of my first job, I remember saying, "I want a job where I have to read the newspaper every day." That was a clue to my future employers to keep me challenged and involved with what was happening around the world. The idea of needing to read the newspaper every day was my way of signaling that I wanted to be forced to be a part of the global community around me and, as we'll discuss later, it's one part of the reason Urnex expanded internationally. Every person you meet offers clues to what is important to them.

Outside of understanding customers, the area where knowing my audience has helped me the most is with employees... and it can help you as well. Working hard to understand what your employees want will enable you to position your desires in a way that makes it more appealing for them to work with you. It's about how to build a team that can collaborate with you and be aligned along the goals you've defined. You won't always understand them perfectly, but your attempt to listen and not just hear your employees will benefit the business.

TALENT DISCOVERY

Some would argue that the hardest part of growing a business is finding people to grow with you. You can't build a great business alone. You need a team. You can be the captain but you can't be the imposing dictator. If you do everything yourself, you'll never achieve the scale you expect. It's the difference between building an okay business and one that is extraordinary.

Step one in talent acquisition is identifying great people, but what does that mean? In the early stages of growing the business, I sought out intelligence over experience and recruited based on what I believed was important to the candidates as I listened to them share their previous experiences. When we were a tiny team, I was just looking for people who could help me use my time and energy most efficiently. I also wanted to find people I enjoyed being around.

Let's face it: we spend more daytime hours with our co-workers than we do with our families. As we grew, I sought to fill more important positions with people who had "plug and play" industry expertise and skills. These were people who could have an immediate impact on the organization from day one and didn't need to learn the job, only our way of approaching it. With any type of hire, I wanted fresh ideas, enthusiasm for learning, writing skills, and confidence more than I wanted preconceived opinions about how to do things. Regardless of the position for which a candidate was being considered, I ended every interview with one simple question: "What do you do for fun?" Listening to their answers to this question always gave me a sense of the person, their confidence, and their priorities that never failed to prove to be of value.

AVOID TOO MUCH, TOO FAST

I believe in planning and preparing as much as possible. When

we got large enough to have an organizational chart, I started creating it not just of the present, but also one for the future. We included shaded boxes with positions we dreamed we would one day be able to afford to fill. Every element of looking at the organization and the staff requires planning for the growth and scale you expect. Although armed with a vision of what a future team might look like, I never sought to fill in the empty boxes all at once. I never hired more than one key person at a time; too much, too fast, seemed a recipe for distraction.

Our philosophy of efficient, focused, controlled sales growth aligned with our hiring patterns. In building the Urnex team, each of our many great people joined in his or her own window of time and each became the focus of the entire organization during their onboarding. Each person needed to be understood and listened to in a personal way so that they could fully absorb our One Thing and internalize our plan and their role.

This step-by-step approach might not be the most efficient, but it was all I could handle. I was determined to pass my business philosophy along to the core team with precision and sincerity. In a strange way, this process allowed us to see the benefits from the impact of each new employee in multiple, unique periods of time. As a business grows, I stress the importance of slow hiring and giving yourself enough time to onboard each person. It reminds me of the imagery of driving with one foot on the gas and the other on the brake. Slow and steady without too much explosive change. Of course, this doesn't work when you're an internet start-up hiring hundreds of employees a month, but as you know by now, that model doesn't interest me.

Staggering all manners of things — including new hires — gave me a chance to get to know what was important to each new team member so that I could maximize their efforts, our likelihood to retain them, and their contributions to the business. The single most important thing about hiring new people is the priority we must place on integrating them into the organization so that they can contribute quickly. As each new person came on board, I spent intense hours training them (one might say indoctrinating them!). I transferred my philosophies and attitudes about business and challenged them to understand our One Thing, our mission and values, our audience, and our brand. In the process, we built an aligned and ever more collaborative organization.

Avoiding too much, too fast, got each new hire on the right ocean current and directed on a path to the best environment for development. It also helped them feel special. On their first day, we presented them with business cards, a direct phone number, and a cell phone; their email was already set up and ready to go by the time they arrived at work. These are simple things to execute and powerful messages of welcoming to a new hire; too often small or new employers miss the chance to make first impressions like these.

We also sent each new employee four books, which we sometimes sent to their homes weeks before their start day. Those four books were: *The 7 Habits of Highly Effective People, The Goal, Getting to Yes,* and *Built to Last.* We selected each one because it offered a look into a different part of success in business: personal organization and goal-setting, operations management, negotiations, and the constitution of your business through a well-articulated mission statement. Check them out if you have not done so already.

EXPERIENCED HIRES

Over the course of growing Urnex, we hired two types of employees: 1) Smart, Experienced, and Confident, and 2) Smart, Raw, and

Confident. They were all smart and they were all confident. Some just had experience and others didn't. When it came to experienced talent, I was blessed with several key finds. Three of these people represent examples of the true gifts from the gods (discovered by networking and putting yourself out there) of talent discovery that helped the business grow like a lobster. I hope that my efforts to listen to each of them and give them insights that were important to them personally played a part in how well we worked together. *You can't do it alone.*

SALES — DON

As the business started to mature into Phase Two, I remained the only dedicated salesperson on the team. To reach the next level, we needed more people to keep the bucket filled, but I didn't know where to find them. I had been having success doing it on my own and I was afraid of messing it up by passing coverage of key accounts to someone else. This was my control freak side. Eventually, I discovered one of the most important hires I would ever make. I did so by listening. Don was someone I'd known since I joined the business. He had been an independent sales broker who had represented my father's products (including lemon covers) many years earlier. In fact, soon after starting, I terminated his contract as I was closing unfocused product lines — and he didn't hate me for it.

In the years that followed, Don went on to be hugely successful in selling commercial coffee machines. Fortunately for both of us, all of those machines needed to be cleaned with products like Urnex, so he already knew our customer audience. In *Chapter Thirteen: Outside Resources,* I discuss the importance of penetrating an industry and getting to know a lot of people. Before we worked together, Don was a guy I always enjoyed networking with. His upbeat attitude, intelligence, attention to detail, confidence, and amazing personality would have allowed him to be great in any industry — so he owned the coffee industry. Each of those attributes is key to knowing your audience — a skill I consider essential.

After a successful run with a traditional machine manufacturer, Don took a more entrepreneurial chance and left the security of one job for the excitement and risk of another. He became the global sales leader for a small start-up coffee machine manufacturer making a brewer called The Clover. When I read a press release announcing the sale of the entire Clover manufacturing company to Starbucks, I sent Don a note. In it, I jokingly congratulated him on doing such a good job that the whole company had been sold. He had performed so well that he had put himself out of a job!

Don wrote back explaining that he had been offered a great new position at Starbucks and he was excited for the success Clover had achieved. However, when I really *listened* to that email, something in Don's email "tone" made me wonder what this natural salesman was going to do working inside Starbucks corporate, where there wasn't much to sell. Perhaps by "listening" to his email, I detected a sense of uncertainty in Don. A few moments later, I called him on the telephone and asked him to consider joining Urnex.

At this point, I had not yet come up with the idea of building an organizational chart with placeholders for the people I would hire, but it was clear that Don was someone who could help and who I'd love to work with. Within a few weeks, I had hired the person who would become a friend, a teammate, and a like-minded sales warrior who remains a key leader of the Urnex sales organization today. Don now serves as the Vice President of North American Sales and oversees an extensive team of industry veterans responsible for sales that are multiples larger than when he started. Don lives and breathes the essence of Urnex articulated in the mission and values statements, and he understands the customer better than anyone.

BUSINESS OPERATIONS — ANDREA

The next key experienced hire worthy of describing as a model of how to find great people was also someone I discovered through listening and expecting the company to reach a certain scale before we got there. When a former college friend and roommate heard about my travel schedule and the consistent growth we were experiencing, he mentioned that his colleague from Bain & Company management consulting had relocated to New York as her husband pursued a new career opportunity. At the time, I thought little of it. This call had come while I was busy onboarding Don and working hard to keep focused.

Taking the idea of this hire to the next level felt like it could be a risky distraction, so I noted the comment but didn't pursue it. I had one foot on the gas and another on the brake. A few months later, my friend explained that Andrea's most recent job, which involved telecommuting to her previous employer, had ended and she was a reluctantly anointed "stay-at-home mom" with a Harvard MBA. With networking in mind, Don on board, and a clearer vision of where the business was going, I took the time to meet Andrea. She wanted a project that gave her flexibility and I saw something special in what she could offer.

Within a few days, I engaged Andrea to work on a part-time consulting project for Urnex! She came in to help streamline Urnex's process for how an order becomes a shipped sale, but really it was a chance for us to get to know each other and see if we could work together. I remember describing the project I wanted Andrea to lead as a "How a Bill Becomes a Law" type of project (for those who remember Sunday morning educational cartoons in the USA).

Andrea's three-month project never ended. When the project work was complete, neither of us could imagine the business relationship terminating. Andrea came on as Chief Operating Officer working four days a week (a flexible response to having listened to her personal desires). Today, she remains an integral part of the Urnex organization — but she is no longer working an abbreviated schedule. It was not uncommon for me to say that "Andrea does everything Josh doesn't like doing." In truth, she did loads of stuff I disliked but she did it better and created an opportunity for my talents to be used otherwise.

We were now a real organization and Andrea and Don each took pieces off my plate and helped our team keep moving in the right direction — up and to the right.

LEAN MANUFACTURING / CONSULTANT — WILL

I could go on and on about each amazing employee I had the chance to work with, how each was discovered, and how much I enjoyed my efforts to get to know and understand them. However, there is one more key human resource who is worthy of explaining as an example of recognizing an opportunity and listening to a situation, even though he never became full time.

Soon after Andrea was on board and in place, I decided it was time to hire a new head of Operations and Production for the business. This was during the period when my brother was leaving the business and I was gearing up to figure out how to possibly replace him. I ran ads and put postings out at the top business schools — anywhere I could promote the position with the prestige that the caliber of candidate I was seeking might be looking for. Here again, I was Thinking Bigger.

One resume came in with the most dreamlike background I could have imagined. Will Bachman walked into my conference room and

I'm not sure why I thought I could hire him, but I tried. *If you don't try, you will never succeed.* Will had graduated summa cum laude from Harvard with an undergraduate degree in physics. While at Harvard, he was in the Reserve Officer Training Corps (ROTC) program from which he was commissioned as an officer in the US Navy and assigned to the naval nuclear submarine division. After his five years of service in the Navy, Will spent a year becoming an organic farmer, making goat milk yogurt and reading the classics while also learning Latin-focused ballroom dance — I'm not making this up.

Once he'd satisfied all of his curiosities, Will was hired by McKinsey & Company, where they trained him as an expert in Lean Manufacturing. During his time at McKinsey, Will completed his MBA at Columbia University. After a few more years developing his skills within this large management consulting firm, Will set out on his own and started The Bachman Group.

At the time I met Will, the Bachman "group" was Will. While I tried to hire him as a full-time employee, he convinced me to become his second client and let him work with Urnex for a sixty-day project to see if we really needed him permanently. He was right. The sixty-day project was a perfect way to add a key member to the team and gave me a much-needed advisor in my efforts to build the organization further. With Will managing the search process and me managing recruitment, we hired amazing people to become our Plant Manager, VP of Marketing, and Chief Financial Officer — each in succession. Over the course of three years, the business grew from a leadership team of two (me and my brother) to a fully staffed organization with an executive team of six. Each hire came on board in roughly six-month intervals. Each was a perfect fit within the puzzle.

RAW TALENT

We had assembled a pretty exciting executive leadership team; however, the place I had the most unexpected return was in hiring smart, slightly clueless, but really creative individuals just finishing college. They were people who wanted to learn about business and improve themselves. Early on, we couldn't afford anyone who commanded a significant salary. These Marketing Managers with their raw enthusiasm and attention to detail would later support me as Assistant to the CEO, help Andrea as finance and management associates, and most importantly, lead our customer service, trade show, and sales support teams.

Like the more experienced hires we added later, these team members were all about personality, and their jobs were shaped by factors that were important to them and that could also help the business. I took to referring to them as "personality athletes" in trying to explain their agility and high EQ or emotional intelligence. They were self-aware about what they didn't know but they were also confident enough that they could learn anything if given a chance. They were people you wanted to hang out with and have a beer; they were able to integrate into social settings, and their youth and naivete kept things fun. They may have excelled at top-tier colleges, but now that the education ladder had reached its top rung, they were unsure about what to do next.

I based the model of these hires on what Salomon Brothers got from me and my peers when we worked similar jobs as investment banking analysts right out of college. We had been hired into the world of investment banking with no relative professional experience. Before I started at Salomon Brothers, I had never seen Microsoft Excel or any spreadsheet for that matter — in fact, I never owned a calculator or took a math or economics class in college. Weeks after graduation, I was an investment banker and Salomon didn't care about my lack of experience ... sure, numbers came easily, but Salomon hired me to contribute to the firm in other ways. While I would need to do the analysis that "analysts" did, they didn't doubt that I could learn the skills necessary for the job.

With all the trust and confidence Salomon put in me, I always felt I could have contributed much more had the chance been provided. Salomon dropped me and all the others into a cookie-cutter mold of what we were supposed to do. They never thought about what each of us could contribute beyond the basics that were the same things everyone had been doing for years. That may have been the way it worked in investment banking training programs with a large class brought in each year, but I decided to try to take it to another level. In seeking out and hiring personality athletes, I determined to give them each an opportunity to contribute to the business at the highest level of which they were capable. In effect, a chance to make a mistake.

In exchange for a unique experience, recent college grads committed their minds, their passion, and their dedication to building Urnex. It was a matter of looking outside the mold and filling the team with talent without going the traditional route. All of this brings us to an example of what listening to and understanding the desires of a different kind of employee can do for your business.

A SAMPLE PERSONALITY ATHLETE — CHIP

Chip was a gregarious and enthusiastic recent graduate of Princeton who had been named one of his senior class's "Ten Most Powerful" (I had no idea what that meant but a few moments into our first meeting I knew it meant he was a special guy). To this day, the award sounds ridiculous, but it was an important reason why I hired him. During our interview, I asked Chip somewhat mockingly about the unusual line on his resume. In his humble response, I could see why his peers revered him. He was at this interview to get a job and improve himself, and awards didn't matter. He took the challenge in my question with a confidence and ease that impressed me. I made him an offer immediately.

When he started, Chip didn't know a thing about business, but he wanted to learn and he wanted to live in New York City. He needed a job and was getting scared about just following the path of his friends who were going to start at low-level jobs in big corporations. Since our offices were accessible to the heart of New York City and the nightlife was of high importance to him (something I admired), Chip was all-in to give this new Marketing Manager role a try. I saw a lot of myself in Chip's hunger to learn and to get a chance to make a mistake. In response, I tried hard to give him the exposure and opportunities I wished I'd been given in my first job.

Chip was more than smart, a great writer, and incredibly personable. He helped build the business and he set the standard for seven other Marketing Managers who would fill the role in overlapping succession over the next ten or twelve years. He was all about ambition, creativity, drive, and energy, and that was just what the business needed. Chip took it upon himself to update documents like our business plan and marketing plan after I explained their importance (See Chapter Nine). He wrote press releases, organized trade shows, worked the trade show floor, shipped samples to customers, managed our online presence and even attended a three-day seminar on search engine optimization. Chip ended up rebuilding our entire website on his own initiative to fulfill the standards he'd learned in this course. The increase in online sales was exponential due to his efforts.

Perhaps one of the best examples of Chip's value was his

interest in learning and trying to become a salesperson. One day, he came to my office and asked if he could try to sell our products to a particular convenience store chain he had read about. The chain was based in Philadelphia. I think part of his interest was a free trip to visit a friend in the Philadelphia area, but that didn't bother me. This company had been a target on our sales list for a number of years, but we'd never had the time or opening to pursue them aggressively.

When Chip asked if he could give it a try, he seemed nervous and apprehensive about messing it up. I looked at Chip and asked, "If you screw it up, how much less business will we have with them than we have now?" My attitude was that there was nothing wrong with trying something new since we didn't have anything to lose. It seemed like a great chance to give Chip the opportunity to do something important to him that could also help the business. Chip put together a presentation, contacted the buyer, and eventually arranged a face-to-face meeting. When this twenty-four-year-young kid showed up in the offices of a major C-store chain, the buyer must have smirked a bit, but Chip came home with the sale. Chip took that chance (and many others) given to him to make a mistake and delivered home run after home run.

A CHANCE TO MAKE A MISTAKE

Now you may be wondering: where does one find personality athletes? First of all, there is nothing wrong with telling the world you're hiring. I wasn't ever afraid to tell this to my customers, my vendors, my professional service providers, and yes, my competitors. The idea that you're hiring conveys your expectation of growth and serves to expand the presence and persona of the business beyond its current perception. By publicly sharing your need for more people, you are telling the world you're becoming bigger and growing fast. This all ties together with the concept expressed in *Chapter Three: Think Bigger.*

The first step is to put yourself out there and explain what you're offering to everyone you meet in hopes that they know someone looking for a chance. In doing this, work hard to think about what might appeal to these candidates and those referring them. Sure, people might laugh at the ambition, but if you don't seek, will you ever find? I found the people I brought to Urnex in the early days by word of mouth and listening. Everything related to hiring was done by me or the department head and not an HR Manager, for the vast majority of my tenure. We were out looking for people who we wanted on the team and we knew that each new hire (however time-consuming and demanding they were to find) was the next piece in the development of the team and the business.

Again, I applied the concept of "Think Bigger" to how I positioned the job in hopes of appealing to the best candidates possible. When hiring Chip and his successors, I daringly guaranteed I'd get them into any business school of their choice. When hiring for a Customer Service Manager, I suggested the chance to grow into a marketing role with a presence at trade shows. When seeking a Financial Manager, I talked about a chance to engage in cost accounting process development on the factory floor, or to one day become the CFO we did not yet have. When it came to seeking Factory Line Operators, I laid out the possibility to move into a Production Supervisor or Technician level in the future.

Most of the time, I had no idea that any of these next steps were possible, as most had not yet been defined and the business was not near the size for which these positions would be needed. However, I set the bar high and expected we would reach a scale that allowed growth for everyone. I always think that if you don't expect to get there, your chances of arriving are nearly nonexistent. *Without having a goal, you'll never reach it.* Do you know what you're looking for in your next key hire?

RECRUITMENT

As a company, we always started a job search by writing a short description of the role. Consider it like putting in the work to define your One Thing or writing your mission statement. Figure out what you are looking for. With that said, we did not limit our assessment of people only for the job we needed to fill at a particular moment. We wrote broad descriptions and provided insight into opportunities for future growth. The opportunistic talent discovery technique we used in the early days eventually gave way to a process in which it was more important to carefully define each job. As we grew and became a much larger entity, it became important to enlist the services of a Talent Acquisition Manager or a permanent HR Manager. But in the early days, when you're small and agile, you need people to not only do specific jobs, but also to grow with those jobs. In a lot of ways, the job of the CEO of any business is being the Head of Human Resources and the number-one cheerleader for the culture.

Once I identified talent, I had to sell them on the idea of joining Urnex. This is where knowing your audience and listening can be so important. In my Marketing Manager audience, I could see an uncertainty of what they should be doing in life. I offered these young, recent college graduates like Chip an opportunity to do things that they would not get to do in a bigger company. To the more experienced, Urnex was a chance to be part of a growing success story and eventually participate in the profitability we were creating. I often talked to prospective employees about joining a "seventy-five-year-old start-up" as a way to show them they were joining an organization with stability but getting a chance to participate in fast growth and excitement. I promised them a chance to learn, a chance to build something, and a chance to fail. My sense was that my audience would find a lot of this appealing and I don't think this type of description was always available elsewhere.

Earlier, I mentioned what I sought in a job when leaving undergraduate school. Four or five years later, when coming out of business school (before joining Unilever), when an interviewer asked me that question, I found myself saying, "I want a chance to make a mistake." My experiences in the very precise and controlling investment banking environment made me realize that I wanted to be put into a position that exceeded my skill set and experience. I wanted the opportunity to work on something so far beyond my experience level that a mistake was likely. That's what I strived to give to each of my hires. I was going to put them in a position to make mistakes; I think that was the hook that brought me incredible talent because people who want a chance to fail are the kinds of people who rarely fail more than once. Are you letting your team spread their wings and take on more than they have before?

COMPANY CULTURE — NON-FINANCIAL COMPENSATION

Just as sealing a deal with a new customer or supplier requires creativity and flexibility, so does converting a potential hire to an energized new employee. We are better at selling our positions or filling our needs if we think about what the audience finds important. One example of responding to what people want is to take a fresh approach to the work week. Multiple times, we hired four-day-a-week employees, which is a powerful recruiting technique. In fact, two of those I hired under such a condition were such firecrackers of intensity that I found myself looking forward to being in the office on Fridays when they were both absent! Friday became the one day of the week I had a chance to catch up on work without the exciting but exhausting daily interactions with each of them.

Both of these four-day employees were women and both had professional and academic experiences well above what one would expect to find at what was then a very small business. For example, Andrea, mentioned earlier, was a Cornell undergrad with an MBA from Harvard and years of experience at the prestigious Bain & Company. Our outstanding VP of Marketing also had similarly impressive undergraduate and graduate degrees. Before joining Urnex, she had worked at major consumer product marketing companies. Neither joined Urnex because it was a big, well-known, prestigious company. I believe they came for the experience and opportunity to work on a team and build something together.

In filling any job, you need a job description for what the person is going to do, and a story about the environment you're offering. Of course, you also have to come up with the benefits that you will provide — and not only the financial ones. There is a lot to offer in the world of "non-financial" compensation. People want to hear about job flexibility, travel opportunities, and little perks like meals out or free coffee. To me, family is very important and I made a point of letting people know that it was okay to leave the office to attend a parent-teacher conference or a child's musical performance as long as they felt they were not doing so in a way that hurt the business. Heck, one reason I was in the business was that I so enjoyed my father's availability to coach my Little League teams when I was a child. That was part of my dream job and what I hoped would be appealing to the top talent I was seeking to hire. The flexibility I allowed is a risky approach, as occasionally, people abuse it, but my teams always honored the essence of the approach and we all got to attend a lot of special, personal events.

One other thing I learned is that no matter how big or small your company may be, people like one-on-one time with the CEO. While it is time-consuming, it is greatly appreciated and keeps you aware of your audience and ahead of problems or unexpected departures. I often would invite all levels of employees to sit for a coffee, take my dog for a walk with me, or just chat about something we were working on or they were doing personally. I regularly spent time on the production floor packing cases for a few minutes or wrapping a pallet or two just to interact with the team.

When conducting one-on-ones with factory employees, I liked to do so without their supervisors present (I know this is risky in a large organization where some supervisors will feel undercut, but my style and trust in all allowed me the chance to get to know the entire team and not only hear about people through the layers of the organization). More than once, a Spanish-speaking employee and I huddled around a computer screen using Google Translate to discuss things. And of course, people want to be appreciated. I strove to record peoples' work anniversaries and birthdays and jobs well done by personally congratulating them, writing them a note, presenting an engraved plaque, or announcing a milestone to the entire organization.

When you know your audience, you know that people like to be recognized and remembered. This is textbook stuff, but we don't always remember to do it. You'll have to develop your own style and list of what feels right for you. Don't ever forget the value of the non-financial compensation. Aside from saving the company's cash resources, it is a powerful currency for team-building and retention.

Awareness of those around us seems so simple but too often we get consumed by our own sense of self-importance. Even the most humble of us just gets busy and overwhelmed trying to keep ourselves on track. In the process, we find ourselves stuck in a hole alone and disconnected from all the resources around us that we've hired to help and support us. By taking the time to connect with and listen to as many people in the organization as possible, we can engage them and build a true team.

- **You can't do it alone.**
- **If you don't try, you will never succeed.**
- **Without having a goal, you'll never reach it.**

CHAPTER SEVEN

MOLTING PAINS: PEOPLE

As business owners, we have to remember that employees sometimes succeed and sometimes fail. In dealing with employees, we are usually dealing with the most dramatic and complicated part of the job. For me, some tough employee matters felt like a molt. The process of molting can give us a great way to understand and prioritize what it takes to keep moving forward in our quest for extraordinary success.

When molting, a lobster removes its entire body from the shell by slowly squeezing and pulling each body part out. During this process, a lobster's gills stop working until the animal can regenerate those vital organs. Lobsters have about thirty to forty-five minutes to complete the molting process in time for their gills to resume operation. During the molting process, a lobster must pull its large claws through the knuckles (which are so delicious but difficult to break open, and very small — think of those little metal pokers a restaurant gives you to work on this area). At times, it has to choose to shed a claw to free itself from the shell with enough time to get the gills working again. This is one seriously dramatic life experience.

Just as lobsters that have lost a claw have the ability to regenerate a new one, businesses can regenerate and reorganize their teams. Sometimes a business leader has to make tough decisions about people to shed. Growth involves the process of expanding and enlarging your physical stature, but it also involves rebuilding and expanding yourself and your organization to move forward.

KEEPING UP WITH GROWTH

This might sound a bit harsh, but I believe you have to recognize that someone may be right for the business at one particular point in time, but not another. When you hire them, you also know that they might not make the whole journey. Many times, I was aware that they might be only a short-term solution. And the truth is, you don't need to hire someone who will be with the business for ten or twenty years — that isn't necessarily the best for them or for you. I always looked for a minimum of two to three years out of most employees and was willing to offset the inefficiency of training someone for a short-term role with the value I expected to extract from them due to their enthusiasm at the novelty the job provided.

Somehow, you know that the business will grow so fast that it might outgrow certain people. What is important is to look for the best talent for the moment. Of course, I never hired someone with the expectation that they would fail or become dispensable, but I was never afraid to recognize that as the business grew, some people couldn't keep up with the growth.

When I found my first finance leader, for example, the business wasn't ready for the investment of a CFO. I hired a talented controller (someone who does the financial work but doesn't contribute the strategic thought that a Chief Financial Officer might). I worked with this person for a few years. I had hoped they would grow into the CFO role, but when it was apparent that they would not, we were ready for the next shell or the next skill set. This person, like others in a similar situation, had done nothing wrong other than existing in a business that outgrew them. I worked hard to give them opportunities to grow and evolve. This is a tough concept to digest, yet you have to be aware that one day you may need to figure out how to let someone go.

Of course, the reverse is often true as well: sometimes people outgrow the business and decide they want to leave before you want them to go. When I was recruiting, I always left the door open for my personality athletes to move on when the time was right for them to go to graduate school, start their own business, or move into a related field of expertise that we were not currently hiring for. These special employees stayed between one and five years. While the old-school philosophy on business and employment may be that employees are looking for a job for life, this is no longer the reality.

I happen to believe that employees deliver the most value to an organization in the period from six or eight months after they start until a little after their three-year anniversary, when some start to either take it easy or think about what's next. The workplace is filled with people looking for the next best job. Your employees are always ready to leave you and that is just the way the labor market has evolved. Companies need to be aware of this and be willing to hire with the idea that the new person has a limited useful life and that is not necessarily a bad thing. This is another place where the concept of "Know Your Audience" and understand their motivations can help you anticipate the need to pre-empt a departure or provide an incentive.

In either case, whether an employee leaves you or you terminate them, it doesn't negate the entire history of the relationship. The employee may still have contributed huge value to the business and their employment could have been a positive experience for all concerned. The work done by one employee is built upon by their successor.

DON'T BE AFRAID TO SHED THE CLAW

Just like a lobster grows out of its shell, the organization sometimes outgrows a team or an individual. There may be employees who have served the business well for years who can't keep pace with the change. It just happens that some people are not right for the place you're trying to go. This is difficult on many levels. However, if it's obvious to you, it's also probably obvious to them. They are unhappy because everyone knows when they are no longer a part of the team or contributing as they once did. In some ways, you're doing them a disservice if you prop them up and keep them around when it's not right.

I often spoke to my team about how much they deserved to be surrounded by great people to help and collaborate with them. Each time I identified someone who wasn't pulling their weight, I spent the time necessary to try to train and develop and coach them. However, at a certain point, it became clear that letting someone go was the right decision for the business, as a weak performer causes discontent throughout the entire organization. Many times, I didn't have to fire these people. They would just kind of figure it out on their own. Rather than agonize, I realized during moments like these that when someone I wanted to leave decided to go on their own, I knew my shell was hard and things were going in the right direction.

That is the best-case scenario. If that doesn't happen, you will need to let someone go. Now I must admit, I have (too) often followed the "good guy" model of business where employers feel obligated to leave a person in their position long after that job has ceased to be a fit for them because they've made great contributions in the past and are solid human beings. Somewhere along the line, I learned that when you know it is time to fire someone, you should just do it. The longer you wait, the less value you'll get in return. It hurts, but if you know your objective clearly, it makes perfect sense and feels right after the deed is done.

Early in my career, I often knew that letting someone go was the right move for the company weeks or months before I took action. I remember being up all night stressed about what it would mean for the employee, his or her family, and the rest of the organization. Those moments of hesitation never felt good, and during that period of weeks or months, I was often passive-aggressive toward the employee. This meant I excluded them from key projects, rejected their suggestions, and in the end, I didn't get all I could from them, yet I continued to pay their salary. Have you ever felt this way?

My inaction and insecurity simply did a disservice to the business and to the employee's high-performing peers who were burdened with dead weight on the team while I sought the courage to take action. As an employer, you have a responsibility to your other employees, your shareholders, your customers, your vendors, and your family to make a change when a change is necessary. Once you recognize this and come to peace with the idea that you are running a business to make money and move forward, the trauma of termination becomes one more step climbed in the path of business growth. If you can recognize that an organization with unequal levels of contribution from its employees can be crippled by a lack of cohesion, you will know the right actions to take.

THE IMPORTANCE OF FAIRNESS

Once I decided an employee had to be let go, I thought hard about how to do it right. I'm a pretty frugal guy, but I always believe I handled severance fairly, and that I gave courtesy and respect to those terminated. This is the right thing to do. It supports the idea of liking to sleep at night. Taking action solves a lot of problems. Everyone in the organization is watching every move you make as a leader. If you do the right thing for those leaving the organization, those who remain gain confidence that you will do the right thing for them should their situation change. Everyone is affected — either motivated or demotivated — by your actions. Just as you work hard to know your audience, the organization knows and watches you.

Once an individual worked for me who was what many would consider eccentric: crafty to the point of ingenious but a terrible communicator, and even worse at working on a team. With that said, he paid for his salary three to four times each year by finding cost savings or implementing new programs. By learning to understand his traits, listening, and thinking about him as my audience, which we discussed at length in the previous chapter, I figured out how to give him the attention and direction he needed to succeed. With that guidance, he contributed dramatically to our consistent, controlled growth. Do you have someone who works well with you but not with others?

Once I left the company but remained on the Board, the leaders who succeeded me were involved in running a much larger and very different company. They had different ideas about how to use employees, and as a result, they were unable to get the return they needed from this employee. There came a time when the employee didn't adjust or evolve, and he was no longer necessary to the business. While many would have expected me to fight to retain this long-time teammate who had become a friend, I operated with what I like to think of as a non-emotional mindset. I knew the termination as the best thing for the business. At the same time, I stressed (with total agreement from our leaders) how important it was to offer him the proper severance package and the respect owed to him in terms of how they communicated. The leadership team was all on the exact same wavelength and this was just one of many interactions where I knew I had brought in the perfect partners.

In business, we must always be sure those leaving (unwillingly) are fairly appreciated for their years of service and that they are terminated in a way that is neither detrimental to the company (from a legal perspective) nor in how it reflects on the company. These became the questions:

- What message were we sending when we let go of one of our longest-standing employees?
- Was he being treated fairly?
- Did the company position itself well in the minds of other people who might feel vulnerable?
- How would this departure be perceived by the industry, our customers, our suppliers, and anyone else the terminated employee interacted with?

All of this thinking involves stepping outside of one's own mindset and imagining what our audience would perceive in our actions.

WHEN SOMEONE LEAVES ON THEIR OWN

In the growth of a company, there will be times when employees decide to leave unexpectedly. You may be disappointed because they are valuable contributors, doing great work at their assigned jobs, and wonderfully handling the "stuff" that comes up in any office environment. You are also probably reflecting on the time and effort you have invested in training and developing them, and all of it is about to walk out the door.

If they are good and leaving for more money offered by someone else, *Pay Them*. Try to keep them. The disruption to the business from a departure of a well-functioning member of the team and the need to retrain someone new is often worth paying up to avoid. This is annoying and might turn your stomach, but if you separate your emotions from your role as the leader of the organization, you'll see that it's the right move. It may cost more in the short term, but the unexpected problems that come with trying to replace someone great can really add up. Have you been in this situation?

If they are truly leaving the team for no fault of your organization, I have a strong feeling about how to see someone off. If they are leaving to have a baby, relocating for personal reasons, or have been accepted to graduate school, praise and compliment and celebrate with them. However, when people leave for another job or a higher salary, I regularly wished them well but forbid the company from throwing a party or a farewell lunch. I picked up part of this concept from something I read about how Michael Bloomberg ran his business, and I found myself agreeing with it completely.

To me, these people were leaving the business and putting an additional burden on the colleagues they were leaving behind. They were not doing anyone any favors and I saw no reason to celebrate their decision to abandon ship. I wanted my team to know that we all worked together and when one person decided to leave us, that was not something to be celebrated as it distracted from our goals and collective ambition. I know that many of these people who left were treated to a private lunch off-site (which was kept a secret from me), and that's fine. But I was not going to run an organization that applauded those who chose to leave their team behind. When someone leaves, your job is to figure out how to fill the void they create. *Look forward, not back.*

BACKFILLING AND ELIMINATING WORRY

One idea that I always held in mind when letting an employee go or being faced with an employee who resigned unexpectedly was something I discussed with Dave, my "soap all goes down the drain" Unilever colleague. When I expressed my concern about how our team would manage when an important member moved on, he told me to put my finger in the glass of water that happened to be on my desk at the time. Next, he told me to pull out my finger. ... He then looked at me and said, "See how quickly the hole fills up? We'll be fine."

I adopted that philosophy throughout my career and learned to give up my concerns about what the loss of any single team member would mean. I learned to expect that those around would rise to the occasion and fill in the hole. Sometimes this meant hiring the next person to do a job before a current one leaves — what can be called backfilling. Backfilling refers to the idea of going out and hiring someone who can rise within the organization for an opening you anticipate in the future. Perhaps it is someone who can take over the job of an employee to whom you just gave a raise (at gunpoint, if that person threatened to leave again). I often went out and hired someone for a lower-level job than the person I was worried might leave, with the idea that the new hire could grow into the larger job down the road. This comes back to planning and preparing for the future based on the mission statement and creating that organizational chart with positions plotted for the future.

A lot of my motivation and mentality about how to run and build a business has to do with minimizing points of vulnerability (those moments just after molt). I was always assessing the business and my team to see where we might fail and working to shore up one spot or another as a way to protect the business from gaps. In effect, anticipating, planning, and preparing for the next molt. But along the way, I also learned how not to worry. Consuming valuable energy worrying about the people problems you have to fix leaves you less capable of focusing your mind on the actual resolution.

(•   **Look forward, not back.**

CHAPTER EIGHT

AVOID WASTE

Avoiding waste is important to a business's chance of success at any stage of development. The significance of each percentage of eliminated waste increases as the business grows and you are saving off a bigger base. Small, incremental cost savings can create exceptional value. When a lobster sheds its shell, it must consume an enormous amount of energy. During this process, waste of any scale can mean the difference between a successful molt and failure (e.g., death). As Professor Tlusty has pointed out, "Molting is super energy expensive." In its effort to rebuild the hardness of its new shell, a lobster is known to eat its old shell for the calcium enrichment. In devouring its own discarded casement, it is, in effect, consuming waste and bettering itself for the future -- call it avoiding waste.

The idea of optimally utilizing all our resources can point the way for us to learn about how to run a lean operation. Some of us may be born having waste aversion as part of our DNA or upbringing; we may naturally avoid wasted effort and repetitive actions that could be solved by better organization and planning. Some of us might figure it out along the way when we see how well efficiency works in giving us extra time to get more done and create more value. Regardless, waste avoidance is an essential part of building an extraordinary business.

Personally, I have an innate appreciation for efficiency and I work hard toward waste reduction in all phases of life. Looking back on the fifteen years we used the Urnex mission and values statements to guide the business, the only two words we added were *"Avoid waste."* We had omitted this concept from the original document for no reason other than it didn't occur to us originally. However, over the years of managing the business, it became clear that not only had we become good at avoiding waste, but doing so was also a business advantage. Reducing waste helped expand our operating profit margins as topline sales increased.

At the time, we were also considering offering an environmentally responsible product. The two words "avoid waste" helped us fit the traits of the business and the new product concept into our core identity and keep moving forward. So, to codify our efforts and encourage more of them, it felt right to add this tenet in the steps toward consistent and deliberate business growth. We made the amendment to the constitution but only after long and deep thoughtfulness.

A SIMPLIFIED CONCEPT OF LEAN THINKING

Lean thinking can be studied in great depth as both an academic and a practical discipline. I was fortunate to have connected with Will Bachman and his Lean expertise. However, I do not seek to present myself as an expert on the topic. I'm not a "Toyota Way" guy with a black belt in Lean operations, and other than a few operations classes in business school, I was never trained in the discipline.

However, just like I cherry-picked the best and most practical concepts from books like *Built to Last*, I have developed my own interpretations and highlights from books like *The Goal, Toyota Way,* and others. As noted, I still recommend *The Goal* to this day as a wonderful way to take complex academic principles of throughput and operational efficiency and put them in a familiar and easy-to-understand model.

Lean thinking is a philosophy with many interpretations. When it is used to describe areas for improvement in a factory, the term "lean" is very specific and requires an all-in approach to doing it right. If you're looking to implement a Lean manufacturing system, there are highly detailed approaches to follow. This might benefit you if you have an organization ready for that level of commitment.

When I joined, the company was not focused on operational efficiency. Over time and with growth and focus, we moved to a place where our systems and protocols were professionalized to standards appropriate for our scale. We passed food safety audits, third-party surprise visits, and collected data and records equivalent to what you'd expect from a global leader. However, we were never full-on Lean in the academic sense. We found a spot in the middle by hiring experienced people and giving them the freedom and opportunity to shape the business in their own ways. Most importantly, we listened to our customers and invested in the things we needed to do to profitably fulfill their requests. By making these improvements, we also made ourselves more efficient.

I caution you that taking pure lean thinking to the "nth" degree can lead to stress and wasted effort as one strives to reach an ultimate level of precision. Unless you're ready for true, capital L, textbook Lean, I prefer to apply the idea of lean as being about generally finding waste in your systems or processes and driving out as much as you can. For most companies, it's not about shutting down a production line or call center every time an anomaly is discovered (as they do at Toyota). Thinking smart and using your resources without waste can apply to the manufacturing floor, but it can also apply to enhancing communication (internal and external), purchasing the right equipment, and designing an optimum office flow — to name a few areas.

Thinking lean is not only about production; it can apply to any clever decision-making that avoids waste, from making sure that directions for visitors are posted on the website and available in printed form on each employee's desk, to daily huddle meetings where the CEO is relieved of having to tell his team what other members of the organization are doing. Reducing waste — and everyone has waste — is key to a business's success. Any chance you can find to eliminate the need to do the same thing twice is a chance to make your business leaner and more efficient. What do you do over and over that you could find a way to reduce or eliminate?

EFFICIENT THINKING

To briefly introduce lean thinking and waste avoidance both for a factory and supply chain, as well as for an office workflow or service industry, it might be useful to reflect on a simple exercise that is often completed in operations management classes in business school. This could feel a little manufacturing- focused, but trust me, anything that flows through an organization from person to person or location to location can be made more efficient by an understanding of pacing and how each step of a process influences the next.

In the exercise, each seat in a row of a long lecture hall (perhaps fifteen to eighteen seats across) is assigned a task in the manufacture and assembly of a paper house that consists of a number of smaller sub-assemblies of paper pieces like a folded roof, a picket fence, etc. This exercise has steps that are assigned to each seat in the row — each seat represents a succession of the process. The responsibilities involve folding paper, connecting pieces of paper that have been folded by those upstream, and other assorted tasks like punching a hole or tearing off excess paper around a perforated die cut. The teacher controls the exercise by releasing a certain number of components at the upstream point in the production line and initiates production by having the first person begin his/her task, and then when it is completed, sending it further down the line.

What students quickly realize is that not all tasks take an equal amount of time, and that when you run a downstream manufacturing line, a call center, a quality lab, or just about any area of business dependent on a preceding action, many people wait for the parts ahead of them to be completed or passed along. Many of those responsible for parts of the process sit and wait for upstream tasks to be completed, and the line bogs down with backlogs, delays, and long periods of wasteful inactivity. *The waiting time is the wasted time.*

A simple exercise like that of the paper house gives you a quick sense of how to think about the leanest and most efficient way to complete a range of tasks. What tasks can be done simultaneously? Where are things piling up? Reducing the waiting time of one person saves minutes. Reducing the waiting time of many people saves many minutes.

LEAN COMMUNICATION

Take communication, for example. In general, I heartily endorse the idea of communicating above expectations — we put it in our mission statement. To me, communication is the essential focus of business success and avoidance of waste. If you can convey positives and negatives clearly and professionally in a way that avoids the need to re-explain a concept or give direction twice, you have gone a long way toward presenting yourself and your organization at a standard well above the norm. More importantly, you save time and keep the workflow moving.

In the context of business management, communication is at the foundation of a lean approach because without it, an organization loses valuable time that could be contributing to progress. No matter the audience, your top priority should be giving everyone around you as much information as they need from you as quickly as possible, whether a junior resource is awaiting your feedback or you are interacting with customers or suppliers. Delaying your responses leaves those around you with an inability to apply their skills or contribute value.

In fact, for leaders, I recommend a prioritization system which involves moving tasks to the top of the list if they include getting the resources you depend on to keep the process moving forward. Put aside anything you have to do independently in order to answer questions from others; when you put responsiveness to others above completion of your own day-to-day responsibilities, you get more out of everyone because there is no downtime without the excuse of waiting on a leader.

At Urnex, I became known for my rapid-fire emails through which I answered questions decisively and directed the next steps explicitly. I tried hard to do this while giving room for individuals on the team to apply their own expertise. Most often, I asked challenging questions that would, I hoped, open their eyes to more possibilities and creative solutions or alternatives. By sending out immediate responses, you get the entire organization moving at a faster pace.

To think like an entrepreneur who wants to build something special, you must recognize that the downstream resource waiting for your response is just waiting (on the clock). It's up to you to introduce the materials into the workflow. Each gap that you take out of the system by offering a fast response that redirects and moves others along becomes one more step toward a lean organization, even if it means simply commenting on a document or acknowledging receipt of information. After the team has their orders and your direction, you are free to get back to doing the rest of your job.

It's not overstating it to say that the biggest part of your job as a leader is to give your team members as much time and information as they need to do the best job possible. Too often, leaders let their egos and sense of self-importance get in the way of the business's success by leaving replies to subordinates for a later time. *No one should have to wait for you.*

VISUAL MANAGEMENT

Clear communications which contribute to lean thinking can exist on a lot of levels. For example, I have always believed in visual management and signage as a way to reduce waste and repetitive actions — and to make the business better. I remember telling more than one Plant Manager running operations to find a way to do his job as if mute or suffering from laryngitis. I noticed that people on our workforce were asking the same questions about their job assignments every morning during the first few minutes of start-up. It was my sense that they were asking because someone was there to answer and because the time spent asking was preferable to going to their workstations.

My advice to our managers was to make a list of every question that people asked, and post the answers on a label or sign on the factory wall with the answers to be read (in English and Spanish) by the people who might seek to waste time by asking. Think about it as a giant, well-organized collection of Post-it notes visible from a distance. The goal was to be able to anticipate and answer every question by pointing a finger at a particular sign. Once a silent reply was received enough times, people stopped asking and started to look at the board instead. Spending a day not speaking is a fascinating experience that may help illustrate the waste in your day — and how much waste you have the potential to remove. Whether you work on a factory floor, in a call center, or on a sales team, try to plan and prepare the answers before someone asks. For starters, think about how many times a day you answer the same questions. Is it often?

One of the best implementations of the visual display concept was a large dry-erase board that listed job assignments, locations, and goals for each day, overlaying magnets with peoples' names onto a schematic of the production floor showing each day's work assignments. There are similar benefits from a receptionist having a publicly visible in/out board, placing an "occupied" light near bathrooms so people don't waste time getting up and waiting for it to be available (airplanes), and having clocks and calendars and thermometers publicly displayed so people don't spend time asking these mundane questions of their peers in a subconscious attempt to distract themselves from work.

Visual management might seem to be anachronistic at times. To help understand the team aspect of what I'm proposing, think about it as a communal visual display. Many members of our team who were part of a Microsoft Excel mindset, for example, loved typed-up production schedules that could be passed around on paper to operators so they could view their daily assignments in charts and graphs. While this information was useful, unfortunately no one read the sheets the same way. And because they were not always discussed collectively, this led to people absorbing different bits of information.

In the end, this meant someone had to waste time and effort getting everyone aligned in their understanding. Instead, the use of a magnetic board, electronic screens, or other large displays/projectors to plan production and communicate ever-changing priorities in a business can get people to look up at one communal display. I'm a big believer in encouraging people to look up rather than down. It just feels better and more engaging. Printing a chart at a copy store costs about $20 but allows you to make it poster size. Whether you use a large digital screen or old-school whiteboards and large posters, the results work! By having a five-minute team meeting to review daily boards together, the entire organization comes together efficiently and avoids waste. I stress the importance of group meetings with heads and eyes raised looking up at a central image rather than down at a piece of paper. When people keep their heads up, they remain engaged and they will make many more discoveries as a team.

LEAN OFFICE FLOW

You can also apply lean thinking to your physical space in both large and small ways. In designing offices or factories, think hard about the movements people make from building entry to their workstations, from workstations to bathrooms and conference rooms, and in our case, the factory floor. Our senior operations leaders sat closer to the entrance to the factory floor, while marketers and customer service reps sat nearer each other. What is the length of the trip people in your organization must make from their workstations to printers and water fountains? Thinking about flow, we should consider the steps one would take from receiving raw materials to moving them to storage areas, and then to production, and finally for the finished product to move out the door to a customer.

As a model, I find it useful to think of efficient flow by remembering the human body. When we consume food, it enters in one spot, moves through the digestive tract, and the excess exits our bodies as waste. There is never backtracking and never a repetition of effort. Things move from start to finish, and very efficiently at that. It can be the same with raw materials if they enter in one place, get processed in a second, and ship or leave the facility down the route with no backtracking.

Imagine the workflow in your business. Are you ever doubling back your steps simply because of the way things are organized or the space you inhabit? How does an order become an invoice? Where do customer comments/complaints go after you receive them? Does the process of preparing a proposal build on the work you've done in other presentations in a way that allows you to avoid doing similar tasks over and over? Have you set up a template for all proposals so that the work you do on one is easily transferable to the next? Thinking about these questions can lead to great improvements in efficiency and reductions in waste.[4]

Avoiding waste is about no longer depleting your energy and repeating actions unnecessarily, and instead, using your resources wisely. This will allow you to grow efficiently across both the top and bottom line. While traditionally we think that reducing waste will only help improve operating margins and save money, eliminating waste will allow the entire organization to grow in every area. Less waste means everything functions at a higher level and we can continue to grow.

---

4 One interesting example of flow is in the coffee bar area of some delis or self-service establishments. Have you ever found yourself waiting in an awkward position for the milk or sugar or a travel lid because the place is set up in a way where you can't take things in sequence and have to backtrack? How about a buffet line at an all-you-can-eat restaurant when there are plates available at both ends? Which is the beginning and which is the end? How do things flow? Do you see any opportunities for waste avoidance?

- The waiting time is the wasted time.
- No one should have to wait for you

CHAPTER NINE

DOCUMENT YOUR JOB

Earlier we talked about how a lobster's inner, soft body serves as the core model or framework for each new hardening shell to grow over and protect. Think of the body as the scaffolding upon which each new and larger shell is built. Just as a lobster's essence is defined by its ever-growing and expanding inner framework, its shell is the structure that hardens around and defines its being, the size of the shelter it requires, and its position in the lobster community.

In the same way, our business is defined by the goals and objectives and priorities we set each year (and sometimes more frequently). As our business matures, we must mature in the effort we put into documentation, organization, and structure. We can no longer make split decisions without asking ourselves tough questions and following a framework to guide us and our ever-enlarging team. We need to be sure we stay on a consistent course and align everyone with our One Thing. We need a platform and structure for sharing knowledge and documenting our efforts beyond the big-picture mission and values statements. This serves both to avoid waste and provide discipline and consistency to our efforts.

At each inflection point, we have an opportunity and necessity to document our objectives and aspirations with clarity. A lobster gets a new lease on life with each molt, and similarly, in each new year or new phase of a business, we have a chance to define our priorities and document our endeavors. Interestingly, just like a lobster frequently molts in the early years of life, your business's earlier stages are when you will want to frequently visit your objectives and aspirations. *When you're moving fast, you have to be sure you don't make a wrong turn.* As the business grows and shells harden at larger and larger sizes, the work going into this documentation gets more substantial and the process slows. Reflection and documentation are key to making sure you continue your maturation.

So what does it mean to document your job? These three major and interrelated forms of documentation will help you plan with an understanding of your own strengths and weaknesses and the opportunities and challenges in your market and environment. All share the act of writing things down. They are:

- Business plan
- Marketing plan
- Project/creative brief

Each of these steps can be broken down to a new level of detail and time horizon, but the concept for each is the same. I am not an expert in the so-called correct or academic way to generate these materials. I freely admit I cherry-pick what works and adapt it to what I see as the priority and the biggest chance to get a return on the investment of time needed to implement things. If you are looking for guides and templates for these documents, you can find many texts to consult. I have always been a "gleaner" — taking the best of what I've read and observed and applying it efficiently to my purposes in a way that helps me avoid waste and gets the essence of the tool into action quickly.

What I share here is my rough framework of the questions to ask and the answers you need to record, and I hope it will become the framework or outline for your system. It is key to understand that writing these down on paper is a tool to keep you on track toward your goals. What's more, documenting them unclutters your mind by relieving the need to remember every detail.

One more thing: I know this is Chapter Nine and this might seem like a step you should have done in the early stage of the business. You should have! If you haven't done so yet, it's never too late. It's a lot easier to skip this step when you're small. Those who try to skip it when they are larger may become successful, but they will never become extraordinary. I included this concept at this spot in the book because when the business matures, you have more information to organize and a larger team to include. As a result, these elements increase in importance and you must elevate the professionalism with which you develop them.

THE BUSINESS PLAN

Everything starts with the business plan. Within a few weeks of settling into my position in the business, I started to write a business plan. It would take me nearly eighteen months to hone it. One way to start a business plan is to buy a three-ring binder with divider tabs (I like paper), or if you're a digital-only person, open a new folder. Start collecting materials to explain and document the following areas:

- Sales and financial data
- Mission and values
- Top customer lists
- Top supplier lists

- Competitor information
- Marketing materials you have today and what you hope to have in the future
- Product profiles, cost of goods, and distribution
- People — Your organizational chart and profiles of the positions

Collect it all in one place and look at it together rather than in pieces. I began by laying out the big-picture overview of everything about the business in terms of what it was in the past and what it would be in the future, both short- and long-term. For our purposes, short-term might be considered from six to twenty-four months from now, and long-term could be from twenty-four to sixty months into the future. The business plan includes all of the positive opportunities as well as the negatives and risks. It is a sort of public and simultaneously private statement about who you are and what you want to be.

For me, it was an exercise in thinking critically about what we had, and gathering all the information we needed to organize the team around a collective mindset. It is the expansion of that concise One Thing laid out much earlier in Chapter One. Doing this work can also help you better focus and define your One Thing. Many times, a business plan is used to raise money from outside investors or give the bank confidence with a loan you are seeking. Sometimes, it is used to recruit a new resource or finalize an acquisition. As we will see later in this book, it may even help you in your exit when you use this material as the first draft of your selling memorandum or pitch book.

Drafting a business plan, a marketing plan, a project/creative brief, and eventually a selling memorandum or pitch book are exercises that may appear to take your eyes off-focus, but they are actually tools you need to maintain your focus. You know your business better than anyone, and getting that information out of your mind and onto paper where it can be shared with your ever-growing team is a major step in maturation. As your organization grows, you can't spend the same amount of one-on-one time with each person as you did when you started. You need tools to share and communicate and involve people. You need to get alignment. Documenting things is one great way to do this. If you have a question or need to onboard a new hire, the work is defined and others on the team can tell the business story for you — making sure you spend your one-on-one time with each team member efficiently.

So, while a business plan might seem like a waste of time if you are looking to immediately energize your business and push things forward, you need to write one if you want to be extraordinary. You might have it all in your head, but collecting the data and organizing it lets you really know what's important and gives you something you can share with others. It will show you themes and trends you might never have known existed. In fact, this exercise is the opposite of waste. We waste time and effort renewing and reevaluating our decision-making when we could have put it all down on paper in a business plan, never to be forgotten.

It is an investment much like mission and values statements that help prepare us for situations as they arise. Take the time to map out your path and your route forward or you will never be sure you've achieved your goals. *Simply put, if we don't set goals, we won't achieve them.* If we don't document what we aspire to do or become, the challenges we anticipate, and the investments we envision as important, we won't have a guideline for decision-making. On top of that, we'll probably waste a bunch of time trying to remember things we otherwise could have had available on a printed list.

ASK YOURSELF...

So how do we do this? Once we have collected the documents and information, we put it all together in a book or master document with words that articulate the answers to a series of questions. Here are examples of topics to incorporate:

- What is the objective of this business? Can you express it with clarity and focus?
- How have our sales been in the past years, quarters, months? Where do we see them going next?
- What makes our products special? What is our sales and profitability forecast?
- What new products do we have on our lists as obvious opportunities for expansion of our portfolio?
- What is our market size? What is our share of that market? Is the market big enough to sustain the growth trajectory we aspire to achieve?
- Do we know our competition? What are their strengths, weaknesses, opportunities, and threats (SWOT)? What are ours?
- Who are our best employees? Our weakest? What positions do we need to fill or upgrade?
- What does our marketing budget look like? Where are we advertising? What trade shows will we attend? Why and what do we hope to get from being there? Are the choices we've made here consistent with the wants and desires of our audience?
- What does our calendar look like? Do we have enough people to be everywhere? Are people going to be overworked? Lose focus? Are they doing enough?
- What equipment or software or other resources do we need to invest in now? Next year? Three to five years from now?

- Do we have a vision and understanding of our best products and the ones we think will provide growth in the future?
- Who are our customers? Where? Why? What risks do we have to losing them? Growing our business with them?
- How are our mission and values statements holding up?
- Have we held true to our initial goals and objectives?
- Did we accomplish our goals of the prior year? What are bigger and better goals for next year?[5]

Next, we organize all of the content and think about it — really think about it. Talk about it with your team, revise it, question it. All of these questions need to be answered but not always to the same level of detail. You can assign sections of the business plan for each member of the team to draft relevant to their roles, and use the writing itself as a tool to focus your organization on the objectives. As I mentioned, once the hard work is done, getting the template in place during the early years — after your lobster has grown in size — you can simply review and revise and update the plan each year and put your energy into the next big thing toward which you will dedicate your energies. With headers in place and last year's work to reference, you don't need to spend a lot of time updating the plan each year. Your best use of time is thinking about what's inside the plan and making tough decisions and implementing each new step forward.

And remember, when used to grow, a business plan doesn't

---

5 Of course, for this, you'll also need all the financial reports and metrics you can learn about in other resources. I don't include great detail on financial metrics in this book, not because they are unimportant, but because they are a given that you must learn and internalize to know your business.

need to be perfect; every last detail doesn't need to be defined. You just need placeholders and thoughts about your priorities and key objectives. In many ways, this exercise can be a confirmation to yourself that you are a serious entity and progressing toward your goals. You are no longer a small player. You are a thoughtful, disciplined, and mature organization. You need a business plan.

THE MARKETING PLAN

What's the difference between a business plan and a marketing plan? In the simplest terms, a business plan is a bigger-picture look at the whole business that includes the marketing plan as a subsection. At Unilever, the annual writing of the marketing plan for each brand was an eight- to twelve-week process that I found painful. The energy we consumed by preparing the details required to satisfy the Board of Directors felt like an exercise in wastefulness. As the Urnex business grew and we attempted to install the systems necessary for greatness, I determined to ensure that these documents had true value. You can do an annual revision to a marketing plan in a matter of days rather than the months I saw it take in the big Consumer Packaged Goods (CPG) world.

Your marketing plan ensures that the tactical execution of your business is aligned with your One Thing and your brand, and that it is relevant to where the business has come and where it is going. In any business, no matter what industry, you need to sell stuff to make money. Spending the time defining your plan will help avoid distractions that amount to wastefulness. Some of the questions you need to ask yourself related to the marketing plan are the same ones in the business plan — with the addition of getting into the guts of tactics and strategies for how you will execute and achieve your goals. If you define the framework well the first time, it is easy to get into a habit of revising and reorganizing your marketing plan annually.

As a bit of motivation for keeping it on schedule, I always used holidays as deadlines for accomplishing goals like drafting these documents. The idea of completing a task or a project before a holiday means that the team is relieved of this project before an extended and mutual vacation. For me, each year, the marketing plan was completed before Thanksgiving in the third week of November. It gave us a chance to buy our media placements and map out our trade show calendar for the upcoming year before the holidays arrived. In many ways, this approach to scheduling also served as a way to build team spirit toward finishing things together, so everyone could get away and enjoy their personal lives relieved of work pressures.

THE PROJECT/CREATIVE BRIEF

The project/creative brief is one more element we execute as a way to document our thoughts and goals and objectives more formally. Unlike a business plan or a marketing plan, we execute this document at a more local and specific level, but it still requires energy and discipline to get your thoughts and goals on paper. Rather than being about the big picture, it is focused on an individual project. The philosophy behind a project or creative brief is similar to that of a good job description. Each is an exercise in thinking through your goals and objectives with discipline so that the organization can avoid future uncertainty (and waste).

Tools are available in other published resources for how best to develop a brief. Following, I share the key headers I was trained to use at Unilever as adapted to fit my own needs. My message is that writing down what you expect from your team or outside resources (commonly advertising or design experts, but the technique can be used for all projects) is a way to avoid waste and get everyone focused and aligned toward the right objectives.

One key takeaway from Stephen Covey's *The 7 Habits of Highly Successful People* is the idea of being the best ladder climber in the world. We must remember that those ladder-climbing skills are of no use if you put the ladder against the wrong wall. Documenting your objectives and laying out your expectations is a way to make sure that you select the right wall to climb.

I'd say that the single most valuable takeaway from my time at Unilever was learning how to write and implement an effective creative brief, and the responsibility that comes with the task. Take some time and think about the following elements to include. A great way to draft a creative brief for a new product or design project is to write a sentence or two under each header and work toward a one-page document:

- Objective: What are you trying to accomplish?
- Target: Who is this for?
- Positioning: How do we think about the audience and what's important to them?
- Channel: Where will it be sold or seen or experienced?
- Image Consideration: Are there any existing concepts or ideas that must be included?
- Look and Feel: Use descriptive words to convey the feel you are going for.
- Branding: What logos or taglines should not be forgotten?
- Technical Requirements: Are there legal or production-specific requirements like materials that must be used or images you can or cannot reference?

- Romance: A romantic and passionate statement about the project that can bring the designer a fuller sense of what you want the design to emulate. Perhaps a story about the history of the product or brand.
- Packaging/Other: Are there things that have to be on the package (weight, contents, patent references, warnings)?

As always, the key is to separate yourself from the audience and think hard about how to define the task for your team, or the resources engaged to execute on your behalf. Know your audience and give them the tools to deliver great work for you. Answer their questions before they ask. On more than one occasion, we wasted time and money by delivering a poorly-defined creative brief to an outside resource. When the design work came back, it wasn't even close to what I had expected. When we went back to the brief we had provided to the designer, we realized that we hadn't done a good job of articulating our expectations. The designer was not at fault, we were.

KNOW YOUR AUDIENCE: KNOW YOUR BUSINESS

By taking the time to focus on documentation, you relieve yourself of distractions and set yourself up to be ahead of the competition. Sometimes we don't ever look at these plans again until the following year. However, if you've done the exercise well, you don't need to. The plan becomes part of the essence of the business and of every member of your team.

Much like the inner body of the lobster, the plan is the part that never changes and upon which a new shell is always re-formed. Well-documented thoughts and objectives become our inner core. Our One Thing leads us to well-defined and clearly articulated mission and values statements. From here, the business and marketing plans become the shells that overlay each new phase of our growth, and are the tools for confronting the world. These documents become our identity, supporting our decisions and determining our choices.

What "documenting our job" encourages, then, is nothing short of a pure, dedicated "self-awareness." This is one more variation on the "know your audience" series we have been running throughout this book: know yourself and know your business. If you apply the same effort to thinking about who you are as I suggested you apply to knowing other groups, such as customers, employees, vendors, and competitors, you will come to an awareness of who you are in terms of both your strengths and limitations. When you are confident and know what you want and where you are going, you don't have to waste time making decisions or evaluating opportunities.

In short, if you can separate who you are from who you are trying to sell to or please, you can come to know both sides with much more clarity. The business plan, marketing plan, and project/creative briefs become the places to put it all down: first to discover these insights and then to memorialize them in a way to use them efficiently to help the business progress. Planning on paper provides relief to the mind and forms a commitment to action. It allows you to take ideas you think about all the time out of your current mental clutter and put them someplace safe where they cannot be forgotten or ignored. This can help you relax while also ensuring that you continue along your path to consistent, controlled growth in hopes of achieving extraordinary results.

- When you're moving fast, you have to be sure you don't make a wrong turn.
- Simply put, if we don't set goals, we won't achieve them.

CHAPTER TEN

KNOW YOUR AUDIENCE, PART III: COMPETITORS

Sometimes viewing competition in the natural world can make us squeamish. Predators and prey compete gruesomely in nature. In terms of the lobster, there is no mistaking that certain members of the community innately seek self-preservation through aggressiveness. They compete to win. Lobsters fight one another by banging their big claws and tearing appendages from their foes. Male lobsters are acutely aware of the molt status of their peers; one fascinating lab experiment caught a second-level male lobster enjoying a nice meal of his opponent soon after his opponent's molt — when his guard was down.

When it comes to business, I'm not a big fan of hanging around outside the cave waiting for someone else to molt. Obsessing about what others are doing can distract us from our One Thing. If we do things right, we get to a stage in our business where we are no longer worried about getting big enough to survive. We do this by being keenly aware of our own goals and objectives. With the reminder to avoid distraction, we eventually mature to a point where it's important that we look at the business market and think about who else is competing with us.

As we think about our competitive landscape, we can learn a lot from the nature of lobsters. For example, the establishment of a clear leader in the lobster community does not mean that there are not always credible and strong seconds seeking to dethrone the champ. Those are the stakes of a competitive situation.

If your business is currently the market leader, you need to know that there will always be businesses coming after you. Alternatively, you might be what Don described for me as an "ankle biter." This is a smaller organization in your market that is striving to gain a foothold in your industry, and doing anything possible to work its way up to your level. Even if you start as an ankle biter, you have to think bigger, as I said in Chapter Three. Recognize in yourself the ability to rise above that status and become larger and more powerful.

Regardless of where we are on the spectrum, we must be aware of the other members of our community and be ready to take advantage of the situation based on knowing them as our audience. This chapter describes the elements you need to protect yourself from vulnerability and opportunistically beat the competition while continuing on the path of consistent, controlled growth.

KNOW YOUR AUDIENCE, COMPETITOR EDITION

By now, you are well-versed in the theme of knowing your audience, but applying this concept to your competitors may be its most counterintuitive use. Why would you want to spend time learning about your competitors? I'll tell you why: it is crucial to success to understand who is in your space, how they operate, what they do well, and what they do poorly.

Those sometimes awkward trade show meetings and

conferences where you come face-to-face with the competition can be a great place to assess your rivals and focus yourself more precisely. Take notice of the products and services the competition offers, the marketing statements they make, the financial statements that might be publicly available about their operations, the quality of their packaging or promotional materials, and the general presentation they make of themselves and their companies. Work to understand the place they seek to establish in the category or market, and decide if you are okay with ceding that territory. I don't believe we can have every part of the market without losing our own focus (much like I don't believe in spreading ourselves too thin in any aspect of business). As a result, your competition has some reason for existence.

It can be awkward interacting with competitors, and sometimes we avoid it. I always felt guarded as to how much news I shared, and I know my presence made them feel just as confused about how to behave. At every trade show I attended, I made it a point to approach each of our competitors. One such competitor always seemed to smile awkwardly, step back into his booth, and stand as if at military attention while I asked after him, his family, and his business. After no more than thirty seconds of trying to engage with him, he excused himself by saying he had to go to the bathroom. This happened at every attempt in exactly the same way. I can understand it.

Sometimes you might feel threatened by a competitor's presence in your space, or nervous that they are up to no good, but those feelings can represent a great time to self-assess and focus. You have a chance to learn something. When you seek to know the audience/profile of your competitor, you are thinking hard about what opportunities might exist for a new or existing business to penetrate the market and one-up you. This can drive you to understand the

market better and accelerate your efforts before someone hurts your business by capturing market share or consumer mind from you.

Do your best to get into the mindset and priorities and preferences of your competitors, just as you do in efforts to know your customers. Look up their office and production site locations to understand their scale; try to meet their customers as much to take them away as to learn what the competition does well. And with the other iterations of the "know your audience" theme, a great way to begin is by asking questions:

- What motivates your competitors?
- What pressures are they dealing with?
- What is their family situation: Are they married? Do they have a family?
- Do they have children in the business or a key staffer who is their heir apparent? How close are they to retirement?
- Do they work well with others?
- Do they have a lot of noticeable employee or customer turnover?
- As human beings, do they appear to be confident or awkward?
- What kind of a team do they have and do they seem happy?
- Do they have other product lines that are different from those with which you compete? Are they focused?
- At what stage is their company in the life cycle of the business?

You want to mentally assess everyone you come across in the business context because that allows you to recognize them as friend or foe, and if they are a foe, how big of a foe are they? Not all competition is bad for your business and not all competitors are foes. Sometimes, competitors are important. They may serve as a point of comparison for your excellence or fulfill a market segment that you'd prefer not to service today. Think about the relationship between Apple and Samsung. They are fierce competitors when it comes to the iPhone vs. the Galaxy line of phones; however, Samsung is also a supplier to Apple. Recently, it was announced that Samsung may make more profit through sales of iPhone X components to Apple than it will from its own line of phones.[x] You can often find ways to collaborate with competitors. Of course, many times, competitors might be challenging you to the equivalent of a lobster duel in the open ocean, encroaching on your territory, and hungering for combat. The more you know in advance about this bout, the better.

WHEN COMPETITORS ATTACK

It is important to anticipate when competitors might be coming after you. Sometimes, the attacks and aggressions might not follow your own philosophy or mindset. It is in this sense of awareness of your audience that you can prepare yourself for what otherwise might be unexpected — call it a molt. I always played a delicate game of promoting myself enough to allow my customers to feel confident they were working with a large, strong, professional organization, but staying under the radar enough to avoid inviting a global multi-national company to invest in new products in the market I was serving.[6] While in some cases I kept my head down, in others I played up my scale in an attempt to offload it in a sale. Regardless of your game plan, sometimes your growth will become

---

6 In the case of Urnex, we had reason to be wary of large institutional cleaning product suppliers that dabbled in coffee machine cleaning products.

impossible to avoid. Figure out how to use it to your advantage.

Remember the image of the lab experiment where a second-level lobster went after the recently molted leader for a meal? After Urnex's brands started going international and showing up in the long preferred markets of our competitors from countries outside the US, it provoked an anger that should not have surprised me, even though it did. Upon seeing our brands in what they perceived to be "their" markets, some competitors felt that we had come onto their turf. In response, they became irrational.

I remember one moment when three competitors were pursuing us with legal action. In fact, this was definitely a time when I felt like I was shell-less. One American competitor claimed trademark infringement, an Australian was working to invalidate one of our patents, and a third, who was Italian, was angry at a linguistic similarity between our long-used (and trademarked) US branding message and their own. All three at once were sending letters written by lawyers, causing us to waste money consulting advisors, and threatening to take us away from our mission and our focus on our One Thing.

At this type of inflection point, you have a choice: you can choose to hide in your shell and walk away, or come out in the open and smile (you thought I was going to say fight, right?). I recommend the smile over both the hiding and the fighting. For one, you now know that you are doing a good job, since otherwise, competitors wouldn't be coming after you. The same can be said of the flattery expressed by the replication of your products, or the similarities between their marketing materials and yours. When competitors start to copy you and complain about you, it is a compliment. But even more to the point, it means they are distracted and don't have a plan about how to run their own business. You've got them more focused on what you are doing rather than on their own objectives. I recommend using those moments to be proud of what you're doing and smile about your success without ever taking your eye off the target of your One Thing.

Distraction is hard to resist at times. It might even drive you crazy not to respond to a competitor's attempt to undermine you. If they are doing so in a substantial way, such as patent infringement, slanderous disparagement, or theft of intellectual property, then of course, you should not cede your ground. But if it is simply frivolous "ankle biting" couched in a marketing message or trade advertisement, then you need to let things go to avoid becoming distracted. In some ways, this is how competition in business is won — if you can direct minimal energy to deflecting and defending against your competitors' affronts, you can benefit from the energy they are expending to attack you. The time they spend trying to stop you can open up great opportunities if you just concentrate on your goals and targets. What you are doing to focus on and build a great business isn't easy, and it can't be copied by anyone randomly. *If it were easy, everyone would do it.*

IF YOU CAN'T BEAT THEM, BUY THEM

In keeping with the intention of knowing the audience that is your competition, I never hesitated to engage with them personally and professionally beyond the simple trade show meet and greet. I made it a rule to meet each of my competitors just as I would my customers. But I also put in the effort to deepen my connection to them. I always let each competitor know that while we might be competitors today, I was available to talk if they had ideas that could lead to mutual benefit and collaboration. Maybe one of us could supply the other with something of value, much like Apple and Samsung.

In speaking, I used vague words but clearly let them know I'd be happy to buy them one day. This served two purposes. The first was to let them know that I was bigger than them (whether or not I was didn't matter). I wanted them to think I was bigger than them through the understanding that I was confident I could afford to buy them — see *Chapter Three: Think Bigger.* The second was that I wanted them to be curious about what I might be willing to pay them for their business. I always thought that this type of curiosity could be a distraction to them that I was more than happy to facilitate.

It was at one of those trade show meetings in April 2005, pretty early in the development of the business, that I went up to the owner of Puro Caff (then the dominant player in espresso machine cleaners in North America as Urnex was still just figuring out coffee cleaning was our priority) and told him how impressed I was with his customer loyalty and the business and brand he had built — I was. I openly told him about his customers that I tried to capture who just wouldn't leave him. I was sincerely impressed and saw no need to hold back the praise. I did my best to compliment his hard work in building a brand and a business I respected. I wanted to make him feel comfortable and praised his creation with sincerity. More importantly, I wanted to convey my own humility by admitting that he was tough to beat.

I had tested and analyzed the Puro Caff formulas, breaking them down and reformulating them over and over. In doing so, we had found ways to replicate and improve upon the product performance. We had packaging that was equally functional and pricing that was nearly 40 percent per unit less expensive. However, we just couldn't capture their customers. It was at that point that I realized he had something that I really wanted and admired. He had built a brand equity that was insurmountable. As I said back in *Chapter Five: Create a Powerful Brand,* the brand commands value and premium pricing. The brand was what I saw as the value of Puro Caff.

I was fully aware of the words I chose and the message I

was sending. While it might have been unwise to tell him what a great business he had built (since it could elevate his expected sale price), I had spent time thinking about who he was as a competitor and what would be most appealing to him. I wanted him as the owner and founder of the company to feel comfortable with the idea of one day selling to me. I did my best to assure him that I wanted to buy not for a quick profit but to continue to nurture the brand he had created. I was prepared to pay a fair price as I knew my business well enough to believe I could benefit from a purchase of his business through synergy. More than anything, I praised and complimented him both because it was sincere and because I needed him to feel safe around me.

It was not the first or second time I had tried to convince him to sell, but it was the first time I put a number to my offer. It was a little bold and I had nothing to go on, as I didn't know his sales or his profitability. All I could do was to extrapolate his profit margins from mine on similar products and imagine that it would be profitable for me to own his business and brand. What was a fair price to this guy? Along with assessing what would be fair, I had to keep his ego and expectations in mind, as I didn't want to insult him with a number beneath his expectations.

From our past interactions, I didn't think he would be comfortable with a complex EBITDA-based price analysis. He was a smart guy, but like many entrepreneurs, he didn't have a strong financial background that I was aware of (see *Chapter Fourteen: An Exit of Scale*). In fact, I suspected too much Wall Street talk would be intimidating and off-putting. So, I just talked common speak and told him I'd pay him one dollar for every dollar of revenue he was generating. It was a whim of an idea but it was enough to get him thinking and a way for him to calculate the value of his business without sharing anything confidential with me.

I knew my profit margins and costs of production. By offering $1 for every $1 of his sales, I created a simplified language for how to talk about paying a more traditionally used calculation involving a multiple to his annual earnings. In your industry, you're going to have a sense of sales and valuation multiples used along with all the technical calculations investors rely upon. My advice is to use that knowledge and turn it into a message you can adjust to the mindset and experience of your audience. Can you offer a price per unit or a multiple to hours being billed? The key here is knowing your audience, and in this case, assessing his/her comfort with financial terminology and speaking in a way that is not stressful.

In October 2005, Urnex Brands closed on the purchase of Puro Caff. One of our best competitors became one of the business's best brands and allowed Urnex to continue to focus on becoming a coffee machine cleaning expert with a scale that allowed operating margins to really increase. This acquisition was one of the most important events in the growth and expansion of the business, and it happened relatively early. It gave us enough unit volume to rationalize significant production automation, and in turn, reduce lots of waste. Having that new capacity then made it much easier to sell to larger customers, resellers, and original equipment manufacturers with newly lower costs.

In many ways, bringing Puro Caff into the business represented the transition from the past to the future. The purchase came just as we were exiting the other ancillary product lines. The small team was finally free to focus on our One Thing. I know that, like the business plan, this happened in the early stage of the business. However, I think we got a little lucky. It's risky to do a deal like this early in your development, as acquisition is hard and can distract the rest of your business from your One Thing. Acquisitions can be great, but be sure you do them when you are mature enough to know how to digest them.

Soon after the deal closed, as I contacted customer after customer to tell them where to order Puro Caff in the future, I was told that it was a great move. These were people who were already buying items from the Urnex portfolio that Puro Caff didn't offer. They were thrilled to get to work with Urnex without the guilt of abandoning this impressive entrepreneur whose brand they loved. By buying Puro Caff, we not only helped Urnex grow, but we helped our customers feel good about working with us. We recognized the intense brand loyalty in the business and added it to our own.

Again, we come back to the fact that slow and consistent topline growth can lead to explosive growth in profitability as a business is able to spread more sales over the same fixed, operational expenses. The purchase of Puro Caff was a big step forward in this direction. It set us up and helped us get to the next phase of business development. The business had another new shell on its back.

)   •   **If it were easy, everyone would do it.**

PART THREE: DOMINANT — CAN'T CATCH ME

PART THREE

In the life of a lobster, there is a time when the animal has reached a size that makes it safe from being caught, either due to fishing regulations or how far offshore he or she finds a shelter. The mature animal has a chance to solidify its position in the world and possibly settle into a routine where the little stuff that was a concern in the early days (survival) is less stressful. While a lobster just keeps on growing at a consistent pace, for a business to do the same, it needs to remain focused on its goals. This is the pivotal point when a business has the chance to move from solid and successful to extraordinary.

During the summer of 2009, I purchased my brother's shares of the business and became the sole owner. The five years we worked together were important times when ancillary businesses were closed, major foundational concepts were formalized, and key investments were made. I now was determined to focus all future investment resources on building a team that could help move the business into the next phase. From the start of 2009 into the next eighteen to twenty-four months, the team grew dramatically. In addition to Don and Andrea, this time period saw us hire the executive leadership team that would be with the company through the sale in 2015.

It was in late 2010, early 2011, that the business moved from one stage of maturity to the next. We were fortunate to have endured the global financial crisis with limited negative impact. In essence, we had matured past the legal limits for fishability and we were on a strong footing. In fact, the economic crisis allowed us to take a close look at waste and cost containment as economic doom raised our awareness of the need to refocus and analyze every expense. Once our customers around the world began to re-emerge from the downturn, the new stability and cost-saving initiatives we had implemented helped to accelerate both our topline sales and operational profitability. Despite the fact that our sales base was larger, we continued to target and achieve a 15 percent growth rate every year.

In this third phase, we had a real business in place. We aligned our leadership, put reporting systems and controls in place, created unquestioned financial security, and established clear priorities for growth and expansion. Scale reached a point where the business was sustainable through ups and downs or molts and recoveries. We couldn't relax completely, but our prioritization system reached a new level. Where at one time, we were concerned about each penny spent or competitive activity we observed, we now only needed to worry about investments many multiples larger or encroachments of a specific size. When it came to people, I knew I'd reached a new stage in business development when the team started hiring people that I had never interviewed, and our sales leaders delivered revenue from customers I was not familiar with.

During this third phase, paralleling that of the life of a lobster, we can equate our business to a mature adult. By no means was the business or I as a leader finished maturing, but we had both reached a new level of confidence. We had found a real stride in our home market and began to work hard to expand internationally. We recognized the need to continue to build and develop the team and also to hire the right outside resources.

Most significantly for me, we experienced a major crisis that we might not have survived had it occurred years earlier. Tied in with all this, I also recognized my own vulnerabilities as I became aware that to be a good leader, I had to let go of some things. In these later chapters of this book, we'll talk about entering new markets, dealing with your crisis, taking care of yourself, planning and preparing for exit, looking at the future, and all those things a mature business needs to be doing. During this phase of the business, I had a team in place that allowed me to step away from the day-to-day in order to view the business from a new perspective. Uncluttered by many of the urgencies of daily operations, I could think bigger, understand and articulate our vision, and find ways to focus efforts most efficiently.

Some theorize that lobsters can live many years longer than humans. They are also one of the few creatures that continues to grow throughout life without ever stopping — much like all business leaders would like for their organizations. Even as they continue to grow, each molt continues to add 15 percent to the lobster's size. In business, most of us hold the aspiration to grow consistently and perpetually. As long as we invest in the systems, focus, and priorities, there is little to say that we can't follow a path similar to that of a lobster.

CHAPTER ELEVEN

GOING GLOBAL: EXPAND YOUR MARKETS

Lobsters tend to like shelters that are just large enough to hold them but not so large that they feel overexposed. As they grow, the time comes for them to find a new shelter. Sometimes, the area where they have been living doesn't have any size-appropriate locations available. Many times, the largest lobsters are found offshore because the areas closer to shore have been cluttered with traps or they have just decided to explore new neighborhoods looking for new homes. Either way, and whatever their motivation as they go out to find larger shelters, lobsters explore new territories.

Out in these environments, they may be vulnerable at first — since they are the new guys in the neighborhood — but as they become more comfortable in their surroundings, they regain their status. Lobsters start to enjoy more or different foods, experience different cross-currents, and learn about new predators that didn't exist close to shore. Through constant maturation and growth, they find themselves with harder and harder shells, a bigger persona, and, as I like to imagine, more confidence.

The growth of a business and expansion into new markets can happen in different ways. Back in Chapter One, we talked about finding your One Thing and figuring out how to grow through focused concentration of your efforts. After putting in the time and effort to assess market trends, understand the industry, and analyze financial metrics, I found my shelter — with no escape hatch — and my One Thing. I decided that branded chemical cleaning products completely focused on the coffee industry were the single target of our efforts, and went through the process of exiting the other product lines.

We had a small but recognizable brand. The first inclination might have been to take the Urnex brand and expand it beyond existing customers with new formulations and applications. In interacting with product users, I had heard stories of how many people appreciated the cleaning strength of Urnex Urn Cleaner when they used it to clean their toilets, their deep fryers, and even the grout on their kitchen floors. The logic might have been to focus on making more soap that we could sell to a wider audience. To be honest, that isn't bad logic and that is a path many businesses follow. However, this was not the route we chose.

Given the anticipated growth of the industry, we decided not to look at making other products for other industries, but to focus deeply on one industry — coffee. We chose to focus our products first on this very specific community. This was different from trying to penetrate multiple industries and learning how to clean a variety of pieces of equipment. In a lot of ways, picking the coffee industry was opting for efficiency. Picking the right industry is just as important as picking the right products, markets, and people. Deciding to focus on coffee represented both good analytical thought and good fortune working to our advantage.

The concept of a local concentration of many products sold to a few customers is different from that of the sale of a few products to many customers in a broad geographic territory. Let's imagine a farmer who grows great tomatoes. He develops a customer base of chefs and restaurants that love his tomatoes. In the next year, he decides to plant cucumbers and then lettuces. Slowly, the farmer grows his business by selling more stuff to the same customers.

This model is not one that I would ever question. It is much easier to talk to an existing customer and convince him or her to buy a new product than it is to find a new customer and start from scratch. It's an enormous investment of time and effort to acquire customers. In fact, keep this in mind when looking to expand your product portfolio — what do your current customers desire that you can supply without taking your eye off your One Thing?

In all cases of market and business development, I believe that we must always remember the value in keeping our existing customers satisfied. There is an old business story about a bucket filled with water. Each new customer is represented by a drop of water you pour in from the top. However, there is a hole in the bottom of the bucket that slowly lets drops of water (customers) out. In building and strengthening your business, you have to work hard to get each new drop of water. While each new drop is terrific, the most important objective is to plug the hole and keep the old customers in the bucket and therefore close enough to you so that you can continue to sell to them, and sell them other things.

It is always easier to sell more stuff to your existing customers — who know and trust you — than it is to develop new relationships. As long as you don't screw things up with missed shipments, bad customer service, unresponsiveness, or terrible rotten tomatoes. If you use your limited number of interactions with your customers as a chance to build toward new and more business — people have no reason to look elsewhere.

I always told our customer service team that there is a limited number of times that a customer wants to speak to their supplier of coffee machine cleaner. Let's face it, we were not selling the most exciting product. The corporate goal was to make sure that every interaction with the customer was an opportunity to grow our sales and strengthen our relationships. Time and interactions spent fixing problems, apologizing, or worse — begging them to continue or resume buying from us — is time wasted. Whichever expansion model you follow, you want to hold onto your current customers while you go out seeking new ones. *The most important customers are the ones you already have.*

In the case of Urnex, we facilitated business expansion by looking at a small and highly targeted product need and finding similar customers across a broad range of geographic markets who wanted those products. We looked at the needs of the coffee industry and tried to find that audience everywhere we could. Our One Thing worked not only in our home market, but around the world.

EXPANDING YOUR GEOGRAPHICAL REACH

One route to boosting the growth of a business is by expanding your geographical reach. For most businesses, geography is a defining factor. It's something like a young lobster not straying too far from its first shelter. He or she knows where to get food and where to run when a nasty predator is coming. It is easier to do business with people who live in your area because you know them as your audience. You speak the same language and live under the same laws. You are essentially living a similar life to them and can relate and communicate to them in a familiar way. You are culturally aligned.

After you have developed a consistent and reliable appeal

to existing customers in your local geography, you may find that the world of technology today allows you to expand and step out of your existing environment to bring your products to new consumers that are similar to those you already serve. You first have to be clear that your product or service can travel well. In the case of the coffee cleaning business and other non-perishable items, we had no natural restriction for remaining in our home markets. For us, people all over the world were brewing coffee and needed their machines cleaned. Before long, we were serving those in our target audience in over seventy countries with the same message we'd used in our home market — and efficiently.

HOW URNEX WENT GLOBAL

Although this topic appears in a later chapter when we are discussing a mature business, Urnex didn't wait until the late stage of the business to go global. In fact, global expansion was a long-term objective defined in the earliest version of the Urnex business plan. With the knowledge that we wanted to go international, we took steps to understand the markets and the opportunities, right from the start. Later, in the more mature stage of the business after we had honed our products and message at home, we got really good at going to market globally. In the beginning, it was an opportunistic learning experience, but those early experiences allowed us to develop a disciplined strategy for global expansion once the rest of the business had matured.

In the summer of 2001, less than eighteen months after leaving Unilever, I started to think about the long-term growth potential and markets where we could sell products that aligned with our One Thing. As I mentioned earlier, we had invested heavily in a high-end Enterprise Resource Planning (ERP) system that could streamline our order processes and systems, and we had developed a brand identity and consolidated message to be one clear, consistent, and focused theme.

We also had established sub-brand names designed to have a tonal sense of connection to people from other markets. Some examples were "Cafiza" Espresso Machine Cleaner intended to build on "coffee," "easy," and end with a *Latinized* "za." Similarly, "Rinza" Milk System Cleaner was about "rinsing away" with the same "za" ending to feel active and romantic. Step by step, big investment after big investment (one at a time), we set up the business to look for the next project. Sounding global in our product names was both appealing to our current market that aspired to do European-style coffees, and had a credibility that we believed would work for the global community when we were ready to go there.

Soon after I entered the coffee industry, I learned that many of our US customers talked about the value of a bi-annual trade show called Host Expo Milano held in Italy. The customers I most respected for their market knowledge had visited the event to meet and develop relationships with the companies that supplied them with coffee and espresso machines. These US-based customers explained how they would travel to this show to learn about the equipment they wanted to bring to the espresso frontiers of America. To them, coffee started in Europe. Recognizing this, I wanted to be where things started. I decided to get on a plane and go check it out.

As I got excited about the trip and thought about what I would learn, I also started to wonder how much good I could accomplish in terms of meeting customers and developing the business by just walking around a big trade show.[7] It was at that

---

7 In October of 2017, the Host Expo Milano Show welcomed over 187,000 visitors from over 177 countries. While it wasn't this big in 2001, it was way more than a high school science fair: http://host.fieramilano.it/en/host-2017-press-report.

point that I decided that if I was true to my model of presenting myself as big as I wanted to be, I wasn't just going to walk around a trade show and learn about my audience. I decided to invest in a booth. It would be a five-day trade show. I later described the tiny exhibit booth we rented as a "veal pen," because it was so small that I could touch both walls of the pre-fab exhibit while extending my arms. However, it served to introduce the Urnex brand to the world and was a chance taken that was well worth it.

It was a big, expensive investment of both time and money. It was a small booth compared to all of the booths around me, but it was a booth and our name was in the show catalog. I later learned that we were one of only two US companies at the trade show and the only coffee machine cleaning product to take a place on the show floor. I'll never forget those five days in November 2001 (just months after 9/11). Day One of the trade show, I sat and waited. Our booth was in a dark corner away from the heavy traffic. Then, at about 10:30 in the morning, a coffee roaster from Australia showed up. He sat down and talked excessively, but I was learning my audience so I patiently listened. I had English on my side and he shared his story of a bad experience importing products similar to ours into Australia from Italy. I showed him our portfolio, and by 11:15 a.m., he placed an order that paid for the entire trip and trade show booth rental. This was one of the biggest orders we had ever taken and he offered to pay by credit card, which meant immediate cash in what was then a very small bank account!

Over the next five days, Urnex would repeat that type of experience over and over. Somehow, willingness to take our One Thing to a new audience led to the discovery of a treasure trove of like-minded potential customers. These were the same types of deeply passionate and dedicated coffee roasters and service technicians that we knew in the US. They wanted our type of products and loved the pricing and the packaging and the branding, and the idea of finding a confident and credible source that was new and exciting for them. By the end of the show and a few weeks of hard work in follow-up, we had received new orders that would become long-lasting relationships with customers in thirty-three countries! We had effectively expanded our market and begun the process of bringing our One Thing to the world. Finally, I had a job where it was imperative that I read the newspaper every day.

YOUR NEXT STAGE OF GROWTH

As our business continued to focus on the mission of offering branded products that filled specialty market needs, we learned about everything our customers wanted and found new coffee-industry-specific equipment that needed cleaning. In effect, we were keeping the bucket full and selling more stuff to our existing customers. A coffee shop has equipment used to froth milk for cappuccinos, make ice for summer beverages, and brew and serve tea. Eventually, understanding our customers' needs led to products for each of these components as well as the development of the world's first product for cleaning coffee grinders — which would receive multiple patents. Our One Thing was helping our coffee industry customers make better-tasting coffee, and we had learned that this vision applied around the world. By staying focused on those customers and that industry, we discovered countless opportunities for consistent, controlled growth.

If you limit the size of your audience or product range too severely, there just aren't enough possible customers in your existing geography to grow the business to the scale you hope to achieve. This is important to remember when establishing your One Thing.

After expanding your customer-focused product or service offerings within your geographical reach, it's time to think about the next stage of growth. While you are unlikely to ever capture 100 percent of the share of your current market, you may have, for practical purposes, maxed out the ultimate potential of your home market. If you want to achieve significant growth, you have to ask of that market:

- Is it big enough to get you where you aspire to go?
- How's the profitability?
- Does it fit with what you do well?
- Is it large enough for you to become that organization you want to act like and present like to your customers?
- When you think about your market potential, where else in the universe can you find similar potential customers who want what you're offering?

Assess the other businesses selling products to the customers you want to sell to. You have likely already begun this work in the previous chapter, Know Your Audience: Competitors. A great way to understand how to grow and model the growth of your business is to observe what the other companies who sell products (not necessarily directly competitive products) to your potential customers do and where they operate. Know your audience and learn from your competition.

KNOW YOUR AUDIENCE, GLOBAL EDITION

Interestingly enough, when you go global, all of the lessons in this book still apply, beginning with the underlying theme of our entire discussion: *Know Your Audience.* In this case, we could think of it as "Know Your Audience, Global Edition." Maybe you don't need to go international and maybe the discussion in this chapter is just a model for how to look at your market and the opportunities in front of you and decide what your next move could be. Where can you find new markets for your products or services, such as new industries or new age groups? Can your product or service be translated to a new application?

I love the story of the repositioning by Pepperidge Farm of their Goldfish cracker snacks from being adult bar food served at happy hours to being food for little kids and babies to snack on. Talk about taking one thing you do well and finding a new market into which to expand! The message is to get out of your comfort zone and expand by finding other places where potential customers for your One Thing might exist. Assess your market and decide if you need to stay close to home or if you have opportunities beyond your current geographical reach, targeted industry, or customer profile.

In order to stay focused on the goal of doing One Thing really well, Urnex had to find more places to sell or else the scale we aspired to achieve wasn't possible in our home market. International expansion made sense for us because we found parallels around the world with what we were doing in the US. We were comfortable in the US as that was familiar, but learning to take our expertise and present our products to a new audience was one key to achieving extraordinary growth.

Can you develop different messages and stories about why someone should work with you? Can you learn another audience and find efficient ways to speak to them? Adjust the value proposition based on the customers' cultural tendencies and you may find an unexpected new avenue for growth. Within a few years after we got serious about being a global company (starting around 2007), Urnex was deriving nearly 40 percent of sales from outside the United States. Today, the brand is positioned to continue to increase its share of the world market while maintaining consistent growth at home. To achieve scale, be bold in looking for new markets and new shelters to call home.

- **The most important customers are the ones you already have.**

CHAPTER TWELVE

MOLTING PAINS: FACE YOUR CRISIS

Throughout this book, we have used the lobster metaphor to describe a business molt and worked to point out how often such an experience may happen during the life cycle of a business. In this chapter, we focus on one particular kind of molt: a crisis. I went through a terrible one that epitomized the feeling of vulnerability a molt can cause. But before I share the painful story, let's revisit author Trevor Corson as he describes just how intense a molt actually can be:

> When the lobster is ready to shed, it pumps in seawater and distributes it through its body, causing hydrostatic pressure to force the old shell away from the new one. The lobster remains mobile and active until the last minute, when the membrane that lines its old shell bursts and the animal falls over on its side, helpless and immobilized. After twenty minutes or so, the lobster's back detaches and the animal pulls its antennae, mouthparts, legs, and claws out of their former coverings, aided by a lubricating fluid. The

most difficult moment comes when the lobster tugs its claw muscles out through the slender upper segments that form its wrists. Before molting the animal must diet away half the mass in its claws or risk getting stuck in its old clothes. Worse, because a lobster is an invertebrate, every anatomic feature that is rigid is part of the exoskeleton, including the teeth inside the stomach that grind food. The lobster must rip out the lining of its throat, stomach, and anus before it is free of the old shell. Some die trying ...[xi]

The moment a lobster sheds its shell is perhaps the moment of most intense stress and vulnerability for this complex creature. Every element of physical protection has been lost and the lobster is a soft, mushy mess that can be consumed with ease by any number of predators. During that week or two, the lobster is weak and delicate as it waits for its new shell to harden and his or her enlarged body to mature and gain the strength to venture out of the cave. All its past strengths and fortitude have been consumed for the molt process.

In business, too, we have moments when it seems we've shed our shells and everything that can go wrong is going wrong, or will shortly. We have to recognize that while we may be entrepreneurs or leaders having all kinds of financial success, there will be times when we're vulnerable, when things aren't working right, and when we need to retreat into a protective shelter and regroup. These Murphy's law experiences are not to be taken lightly — and, more importantly — they must not be unexpected. While we do not know what will go wrong to disrupt our security and sense of confidence, we must be prepared for this inevitability. This is true for all people as well as businesses.

MOLTS NEVER COME AT THE BEST TIME

While it may feel like there is never a good time for a molt, molts seem to attack your business at a time when you are already depleted, stressed, and overextended. When I experienced my worst business crisis, I was already in the middle of five different challenging situations in a three-month period:

1. After having our third child, we moved our family to a new home. I was overseeing the move and my wife was busy with a new baby and everything else that burdens a young family.

2. The home move coincided with moving the Urnex manufacturing facility and offices to a new site nearly three times larger. This involved shutting down one location and opening another without missing any customer orders in the process. (Side note: Don't move your business and your home in the same month.)

3. We were engaging and finalizing the contracts and sales agreements with what would eventually become two of the top ten largest customers of the business. They were such mission-critical customers that they both cracked the top ten in terms of revenue after their first year.

4. My kids were entering a new school, and Hurricane Irene hit during the first week of school. Our new home was without electricity for six days and we had not yet met any neighbors.

5. Finally, I was stressed and wavering with how to manage a new and highly paid employee. He was neither contributing the value nor relieving me of the responsibilities I had expected. Clearly, I had not yet

read Chapter Seven of this book, and found myself
stuck sinking time and energy into managing his role
within the business when I should have shed the claw.

Had I not already been "mid-molt," as it were, the crisis I am about
to describe might have been easier, or maybe it never would have
happened. The business needed me to focus every ounce of my
energy and power on one situation, which, looking back, I now realize
included multiple challenges simultaneously.

THE CONTAMINATION CRISIS

As I previously mentioned, Urnex had just signed a lease and
assumed control of a new facility. After months of construction
and design efforts, we were beginning to build inventory and
stocks to allow us to dismantle machines at the old site and
start the relocation process. We knew this was going to be a
complicated point in time and the team was working hard to *plan
and prepare* for the future challenges we would face. Just a few
months earlier, we had secured a business relationship with one
of the country's largest manufacturers of single serve coffee
brewers to produce a custom and co-branded descaling solution
for sale to their customers. The business relationship was one I
had pursued for years and I was about to add them to the bucket.

The orders started coming in and the scale was like nothing
we had ever seen. One single SKU of product was being ordered
in daily sales volumes that were two and three times the weekly
sales volumes the entire company had experienced just a few years
earlier. We were set up to produce the product and the formulas
were simple. Our margins were more than healthy and our team was
prepared. The orders started shipping out of the old facility and I was
imagining how much easier it would be to continue to fill these orders

once the new factory was in operation. I began thinking about the additional support staff this new business would help us afford, the improvements we could make to the offices, and the weekend house I imagined I would be able to buy. Perhaps I got a bit ahead of things.

That was when an unidentified contaminant was found in some bottles of the product. This led to safety concerns, confusion, and intense scrutiny. Legal action was threatened and in addition to the loss of hundreds of thousands of dollars of potential sales, we were told that the customer had spent nearly $1 million on PR efforts to preempt a negative impact on their business from this event. They made it clear that Urnex would be expected to compensate them for this expense. What was going to be an enormous profit center, the crown of all of our efforts, was a molt in full force. We now had the news media publishing pieces on the recall of the descaling product, and our entire organization was consumed in managing the issue. Our giant, swirling crisis had just made landfall.

THE CASE OF ODWALLA COMES TO MIND

As soon as I realized I had to put on my crisis management hat, I was transported back into a lecture hall watching the body language and demeanor of a CEO who had been through something terrible but came out on top. I remembered attending a lecture presented by Greg Steltenpohl who had been the founder and CEO of Odwalla juice drinks. He had come to the Kellogg School of Management to tell the story of the juice company he had started in the early 1980s with bottles sold from the back of a Volkswagen van. By 1993, Odwalla attracted the attention of major investors and went public. By 1996, the company had achieved roughly $60 million in sales, a new production plant, and owned refrigerated trucks for distribution. I imagine the VW had been retired and preserved for posterity.

Unfortunately, an E.coli outbreak causing one child to die and over sixty people to become ill was directly linked to the apple juice component of Odwalla's products. I remember being completely unfamiliar with this story but amazed by his calm as Mr. Steltenpohl recounted the concept of the business, its growth, and then the tragedy he had to confront. He went on to describe how he issued his first press release on the problem within thirty minutes (look up the story and you'll find it reported that he took only twenty-three minutes to respond), accepting full responsibility and pledging to work toward both resolution and bereavement. He and his team seemed to take on every ounce of responsibility they could — and definitely more than they had to, or other companies might have. There was no ego involved.

Steltenpohl spoke of not so much trying to control the dialogue but doing the right thing. It was his products that had caused these problems and he was out in front, communicating and taking responsibility rather than letting the media tell his story. In many ways and by all assessments, he was overcommunicating. As a result of this experience, Odwalla's sales declined nearly 90 percent. However, the company continued to focus on its core strengths while implementing major improvements to its business model (for example, it previously stressed the health value of unpasteurized juices, but quickly changed that philosophy). On October 30, 2001, just five years after the incident, Coca-Cola bought Odwalla for $181 million, representing a turnaround of unexpected scale and a crisis and molt well-handled.

FACE YOUR CRISIS

From the day I heard it, Steltenpohl's story became part of the inspiration for my approach to business, and later it was a key part of my crisis management mindset. Long before the contamination of our product was detected, I had adopted a philosophy of "owning" everything about the business in the sense of taking full responsibility for both the good and the bad. That was the essence of the Urnex brand.

When the Urnex crisis happened, I took every call from every contact that wanted answers. I reached out, hoping to learn more about what the customer was experiencing, invested heavily in lab resources to identify the source of the issue, cleaned every element of our plant (which we were vacating), documented all areas that could be useful for finding the problem, and never ceased to email and call each contact I could, day and night. I made myself completely available, invited investigators to tour our plant, swabbed our facilities for mold and other bacteriological growth, and basically determined that every bit of what I could do I was going to do. I proactively recalled a few Urnex branded products that might have been connected to the contaminant, even though none was ever found to be impacted.

It wasn't easy. When you have a moment when everything you've built seems like it might come crashing down, it is tempting to dive into your rocky outcrop or cave and hide away from your problems until they are resolved. But companies make a mistake when they fail to respond to a problem in an immediate and substantial manner. *Problems don't go away until we find solutions.* When we step away and hide from tough things, we cause our customer or partner or audience to doubt our conviction and our commitment to the relationship. By failing to engage the customer or the consumer with our involvement in the situation, we forfeit all opportunity to prove ourselves of value for the future. By being in front of a situation, we control the dialogue. We contribute our perspective and knowledge to the conversation.

All businesses make mistakes and have problems. *Mistakes are okay as long as we don't make the same mistakes more than once.* I have found that customers are understanding. They also make mistakes and recognize that the best of us mess up. It is when we fail to admit our mistakes to ourselves or those who they affect that we miss an opportunity. It is during our very moments of vulnerability when we can recreate our message, impress our partners, and build our identity.

I can humbly admit that I made a lot of mistakes in building Urnex. Some were insignificant and others were enormous. In 2011, I clearly took on too much at once. Whether or not the contamination crisis would have been avoided had I been less ambitious, I cannot know. What I do know is that two years after we discontinued the product and lost the account, the partnership restarted. During that time, we worked to better understand the problem. Independent labs confirmed that the contaminant was non-harmful and the issue was only aesthetic. The customer, satisfied that we had handled things exceptionally and comforted that we had not stopped looking for the root cause, became Urnex's largest account. I happen to believe that the reason we regained the account and won the bid to produce the next generation of the product was our handling of the crisis situation, confronting the problems, accepting responsibility, and dedicating all resources to resolution. The trust and confidence built up in that experience through overcommunication and a willingness to accept responsibility led to the next phase of the relationship and served to harden our shell for the future.

KNOW YOURSELF

Crises can lead us to gain an unprecedented amount of self-awareness. As a P.S. to this story, I want to acknowledge that I made enormous mistakes in building the business and taking on too much responsibility. During the management of the contamination crisis, I was driven not so much by a desire to fix the business as I was to keep from losing it. It was as though I was pushing a giant boulder up a hill (a really big hill) and unable to give up because giving up meant the boulder would crush and kill me. I lived under that pressure for a solid two months. Each day and night, I dedicated my energy and focus to pushing that thing up the hill with every bit of energy I could muster.

About thirty days after a press release was issued recalling our product, I began to realize I should have taken better care of myself. Without getting too much into my personal story, I can share that a few months after moving my home and business, and of course, the crisis of contamination, I crashed physically. Something wasn't right. After a number of experiences of nausea and fatigue that I attributed to working too hard, drinking too much wine, and partaking in too many steak dinners, I went to see a doctor. I spent a night in the hospital so doctors could assess my situation, since nothing seemed problematic other than the symptoms I was describing. The next morning the doctor discovered a blockage in an artery in my heart.

I was a forty-year-old, non-smoking male with no family history of heart disease, a regular workout regimen, and a lot to live for. I was fortunate that the issue was uncovered and a stent was inserted before I damaged my heart or experienced a heart attack. Somehow, I like to believe, *I knew myself* enough to get checked out, but more importantly, the doctors did a great job following the protocols and identifying my problem.

Now, the lesson here is that the scare of the heart event allowed me to have a clear focus and understanding of how to continue to grow the business without wasting time. The epiphany of this experience allowed me to do everything I had been doing, but somehow do it more efficiently — avoiding even more waste. When I mentally readjusted to my new medical reality, I ran the business completely differently and found myself overseeing even more explosive growth than we had experienced in the ten years prior to coming through the molt of the crisis and my heart incident.

Once treated, I found myself with time to go to the gym at 7 a.m. each morning when I'd previously been in the office by that hour. I now left the office every night in time to be home for dinner with my wife and children. I learned to silence my phone as soon as I walked into the house and only take a quick check of it before going to sleep, when I could answer a few emails to Asia or the West Coast. I passed up a number of invitations to travel to meet customers and sent members of the team in my place.

The experience taught me to make decisions faster and cut through the dialogue in long meetings. I learned to make pricing proposals that didn't require drawn-out negotiations, and generally accelerated the pace of everything without losing focus on my goal of consistent, controlled growth. I just went after the prize and figured out how to do it in less time and with faster results. We were now a bigger business and our growth goals took more sales to achieve.

It was also during this time that I learned to delegate more responsibility and manage my expectations of perfectionism (I let up a bit on the final precision to achieve a faster, larger scale, and felt comfortable doing this because of the way this issue had been addressed in our mission statement). I relied on my excellent team and worked hard to be less prescriptive and more visionary. It was during the three-and-a-half-year period after my heart scare that the business experienced the most consistent growth, and it was growth on a much larger base.

In reviewing timelines while writing this book, I realized that

I received my stent in late November 2011, and the sale of the business closed in April 2015. In that period, the business's EBITDA and value grew tenfold while we continued on our path of 15 percent year-on-year growth. The scale was leading to operational excellence at levels that we had not previously anticipated.

In some ways, that concentrated period may be more valuable from a business storytelling perspective than anything else. All of this happened without pushing a big boulder up a hill or working long days. My new work-life balance was in dramatic contrast to what I had been doing to get the business into position in the ten years prior. After my health scare, the value of those major investments, the projects we instituted, and the team we assembled became clear. We had created a foundation for a business that could run as a standalone entity. Most importantly, I was mentally free to let some things go, and I found myself more self-aware than ever.

I've continued my commitment to physical exercise and now rarely fail to exercise six of every seven days. This works for me and the numbers attest that it worked very well for the business. I'm not here to offer medical advice but to encourage you to find the value of physical activity in your daily routine. It is important to recognize that being active and healthy is just as valuable to growing your business as is having the best marketing campaign, understanding the customer, and focusing on One Thing.

In these moments of vulnerability, our friends and family, our investment in our physical and emotional well-being, and our confidence in ourselves and our ultimate objective can serve as the rocky cave-like shelter we need. All these elements give us the time and security to allow our new shells to harden as we pursue our path of forward growth and progress. Taking care of ourselves is as much a business priority as a personal one.

- Problems don't go away until we find solutions.
- Mistakes are okay as long as we don't make the same mistakes more than once.

CHAPTER THIRTEEN

OUTSIDE RESOURCES

For a lobster, the ocean is a source of sustenance provided by the wonders of nature. They scavenge through the sea bottom to find the perfect crevices for safety and the ideal foods to maintain their constant growth. To a business, the search for the best industry and professional resources that support our vision is a task not to be taken lightly. It is by building our organization with both internal and external resources that we are positioned to support the ever-greater initiatives necessary for our consistent, controlled growth. In this chapter, I offer you tools and ideas about how to find and use the best outside resources.

Our success depends on the team we build and the organizational alignment we achieve. As we grow, we also depend on a wide range of outside resources. These include industry peers, lawyers, accountants, consultants, bankers, designers, and many others. Each resource is interconnected with how you operate your business, the community outreach you pursue, and the networks you develop. Just as a lobster must leave his shelter to find food, we must also go out into the community and find those resources that can help us.

YOUR INDUSTRY

In many ways, I got lucky finding myself in the coffee industry. Over the last twenty years, coffee has been an explosive part of the global economy, and chains like Starbucks, Dunkin' Donuts, and Costa UK, combined with the tens of thousands of independent coffee retailers around the world, have introduced a new component to the culture of the world through the availability of a social place to connect over a beverage. Just for context, here's a look at the trendline for the growth in US specialty coffee retail outlets from 1991 to 2015. Pretty much the same trendline exists in all developed countries around the world, with China being particularly explosive in the last few years.

U.S. SPECIALTY COFFEE SHOPS 1991 - 2015 [xii]

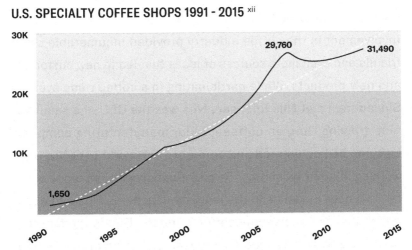

One of the first things I did when I chose the coffee machine cleaning product line as our One Thing was to engage with the industry trade organizations focused on coffee. I started attending conferences and putting myself out there to meet people, find customers, and learn my audience. I'll be honest, I hated it. By nature, I'm a pretty introverted guy who prefers downtime with the family and quiet moments alone. However, I recognized that networking within the industry was a great opportunity for the business.

I attended cocktail parties, fundraising receptions, and volunteered to join committees on any topic to which I could find a connection. Over time, I came to realize that I was the luckiest guy around. The Specialty Coffee Associations of America and Europe (now merged as one global organization) were filled with smart, energetic entrepreneurs each trying to build a successful business. By engaging with this community, members often referred new customers to me, introduced me to consultants and advisors, and gave me updates on new possible target accounts. Friends in the industry regularly briefed me on the activities of my competitors. Are you getting out there and connecting in your industry?

COLLABORATION LEADS TO INNOVATION

Involvement in the coffee industry provided innumerable close friends and even more sources of ideas that led to new customers and new products. While participating in a coffee trade event in Singapore, I met Nils Erichsen. Nils was the CEO of a small but fast-growing German coffee grinder manufacturing company. Like me, he had entered and embraced the world of coffee after working in other industries. Through friendly conversations about our business models and the industry in general, I learned about the challenges of cleaning coffee grinders. Due to the fact that a coffee grinder sits atop an exposed electric motor, it cannot be cleaned with detergent and water, as this would damage the components. Historically, people have ground rice as a way to dislodge coffee oil residue from the internal cutting teeth, but this practice risks destroying a grinder in a number of ways. Armed with this new bit of information and a new friend who had access to a limitless supply of coffee grinders (since I broke quite a few during product development), I set out to come up with a grinder cleaner.

Several years later, in close coordination on safety and efficacy testing with Nils' team at Mahlkönig GmbH, Urnex filed a patent for Grindz Grinder Cleaner. In 2005, a patent was granted for the world's first coffee grinder cleaning product. These coffee-bean-shaped tablets made of edible and biodegradable matter simply needed to be ground and purged with fresh coffee (no water or chemicals required). Not only did Urnex have a major new innovation, but we also had an industry partner in Mahlkönig. Nils and I and our teams would remain in constant contact, sharing trade show booths, insights about customers and the coffee industry, movement of key players from one company to another, and a host of other trade-related market knowledge that is only accessible with eyes and ears all over the world.

This was just one of many fortuitous outcomes that came from entering and engaging with the industry, networking, and getting out there. The point here is that *you can't do it alone.* Just as you need a unified team of employees, you also need industry contacts and partners working in the same markets to really achieve something extraordinary. Think about places where you can get involved. Even if it's not your thing, your business will benefit.

EXPLORING YOUR OPTIONS — PROFESSIONAL RESOURCES

In the process of penetrating the industry through networking initiatives, I also spent a lot of time thinking about whether to contract professional outside resources or tackle projects with our internal team members. As I thought about these things, I had access to the minds of contacts leading other companies throughout the coffee industry, and I could bounce my ideas off of them and ask questions. My network was always there as a sounding board. Growing your business in an industry with peers facing similar challenges can lead to an invaluable exchange of ideas. Do you use your clients and suppliers for advice?

Throughout my earlier professional experiences, I saw (and participated in) what I considered to be deeply wasteful expenditure on outside professionals. Have you ever seen the consulting and professional budgets of a big consumer products company or investment bank? Running Urnex was the first time I was working in an organization with limited resources. I had no idea what expenses it made sense to incur, so I looked to friends and industry colleagues for context.

To start, I learned that you have to understand why you seek to hire an outside resource and what deliverable you expect to receive from the investment before hiring them. Here again, think closely about what you seek and put your goals on paper. Define it all in a brief, and you'll save so much time avoiding a future mess. Here are a few questions to ask yourself:

- What expertise do they have that you do not?
- What can they do better than you or your organization because of experience or training or connections?
- What do they bring to the equation that is new or unknown to you?
- How much of your time is this firm or vendor going to free up?
- What level of resource is going to work on your business?
- What tier of services are you looking for? Are you okay not having an answer in twenty minutes when a lower price gets you the same quality answer in a day?

- What size firm are you looking to work with, large or small? Are you looking for big city or suburban (which might come with a lower cost)?

The non-emotional decision-making we referenced earlier can help you here as well. You don't want to make any of these decisions to select resources with your ego in mind. Don't worry about the brand recognition of a provider if you can get the same value from someone less well-known (see exception in selecting a selling advisor in Chapter Fourteen). You want smart, talented resources that have your best interests in mind and are capable of keeping pace with the speed you intend to pursue in your business growth. Most of all, you want your outside resources to bring something to the business that you cannot or do not want to manage internally.

CAN YOU DO IT YOURSELF?

I'm frugal by nature, and this perspective helped in assessing talent and resources to hire (other times it did not). There are always experts who can do specific tasks better than we can. In evaluating resources, you have to consider the merit of doing something yourself vs. the cost and investment of using a specialist. This is similar to a classic "make vs. buy" decision about whether to create something in-house or buy it from a specialist. You can ask yourself a lot of questions, but the most important one is whether or not trying to do something yourself will take you away from your One Thing.

Can you write and review your own contracts? Should you? Can you start the first draft of a separation agreement or term sheet of a deal to save yourself the hours a lawyer is likely to bill for doing what is obvious to you? Once again, should you? I like to think that there is a delicate balance here. It's one thing to recycle documents you have used before or sketch an outline for a new program yourself. It's quite another to attempt to do the work of a professional. Putting in the effort to define concepts, strategies, and objectives for your outside resources, but then stepping back and letting them do their work, is where you create value.

In working on the two patents we filed over the years, I took the first step to fill in the details of a template provided to me by the lawyers, with as much information as I could articulate about what innovation we were developing. I did this more out of a desire to give the lawyers the tools to take the handoff and put the document together properly. It's a balance between sharing ideas and letting professionals do their jobs.

BUT I ENJOY IT

It is hard to put a price tag on outsourcing a task you actually enjoy doing. For example, some business owners just love IT problems. They find themselves never giving that up and rationalizing it by saying that a third-party vendor or hiring an IT head is too expensive. Be honest with yourself. Are you running a business to pursue your hobby or are you there to run and grow the business? Even if you love fixing the computer network issues, be self-aware as to whether or not this is the best use of your time.

I often found myself on the opposite end of the spectrum. I wasn't personally invested with pleasure in doing any particular task. I was there to grow the business with an undying focus. My priorities were product development, team management/motivation, and customer-facing engagement. I realized that there were a lot of things I did not like doing, and those came off my plate fast to keep me on my One Thing. I could figure out these tasks, but if they didn't excite me, I needed someone else internal or external to oversee them. For these tasks (in my case, Union labor negotiations, health insurance policy selection, property and casualty insurance, hiring and firing, and a few others), I looked to outsource the responsibilities to a third party and spent a lot of money on lawyers and consultants to help me. When I hired Andrea, her talent with structure and process led to an outside resource becoming permanent. The idea of converting someone from outside to inside is worth keeping in mind.

WHEN TO HIRE INTERNALLY

If you are like me, starting with a small but growing business, you will one day realize that every job you get to hire someone to perform is a job or task that you probably did yourself. I started out running finance and marketing and operations and sales and even customer service. Over time, I made decisions about which of these roles we could outsource by using a third party, and which — as in the case of Andrea who became the COO and took over everything I didn't like to do — you may decide to hire to perform internally as a member of the team. When you start small, you go through a process where you may add resources incrementally starting with outside contractors, and eventually move them into full-time staff.

You make each decision by balancing the time you are dedicating to that task with the cost of the new hire. Each new person you add to your team frees you up to focus on the next big thing that can grow the company. But just because you hire someone, that doesn't mean you are now off the hook! You have to work hard to define the job you are hiring them to perform. A job description for a project should be as well-written as one for a full-time job, or for a creative brief.

You have to manage the handoffs with care, thoughtfulness, and a lot of attention directed toward the new person, remembering to avoid starting too many resources at once. Don't hire someone as a consultant or outsourced resource and not give them the freedom to do their job; that's a waste of your money and their time. Having done the job yourself before might give you great confidence, but don't fall prey to the frustration of how much time it takes you to teach someone your job. If you give up and do the job for them, you made a bad hire. *You could do it yourself, but then why did you hire them?*

NETWORKING AND FINDING TALENT

Let's say you've decided that you could utilize outside professional resources to help grow your business. How do you find them? The answer is networking from within your industry, and any and all of your past connections. In my opinion, the keys to networking are confidence and a willingness to ask. Observe people and contacts you admire and ask them how they do things. What consultants do they use? Do they like them? Why? Why not? Think about your peers and colleagues and contacts and ask, ask, ask.

Never be afraid to look dumb because you don't know where to find a good lawyer or how to recruit talent. My most valuable legal advisor in Europe came through a referral from my friendship and connection with Nils Erichsen, who was also my collaborator on the grinder cleaner. Our best packaging designer was found based on a compliment paid to another company at a coffee industry trade fair.

People like being asked for their advice; it makes them feel valued and it expands your network. I often asked customers and vendors for suggestions when I was seeking to hire a new person. I asked the local government, such as the mayor's office, for referrals. I asked truck drivers who came to my factory every day if they knew people looking for work. I sent emails to friends asking if they had friends of friends who might be looking for a job. I invited people to visit the factory and always pointed out new positions we were seeking to fill or resources we wanted to hire.

As noted earlier, I kept an organizational chart filled with a list of open positions I hoped to fill when we grew. It was my way of being prepared to pounce on great talent when it became available. The same can be true for knowing what outside resources it might be nice to find. Speaking publicly about our need for resources or desire to fill open positions committed us to filling them and also let us tell the world we were looking. Once again, we communicated that we were growing. Openness lets you stumble upon great opportunities. Speaking up and raising ideas or asking for assistance leads to great things. *If you don't ask, you'll never know.*

Along with openness, you also need to recognize that not all people are comfortable being open. If your personality is comfortable seeking out advice and ideas, you can bring people together. Don't be afraid to offer names of resources you've used in the past or to suggest a website or firm you have used with success. If you can become a networker offering up help to others, you will surely find yourself receiving advice and resources for your own benefit in return.

THINKING BIGGER GOES BOTH WAYS

If you do decide to go ahead and hire an outside resource, remember that Thinking Bigger goes both ways. Just as you aspire to attain a certain scale, you are looking for professionals who can grow with you as you pursue your aspirations. While you might need one type of work done today, will they be able to help with other types of work in the future? Are you willing to pay a premium for that future potential? Will they be there to help you through your tough times, your molts?

When it came to lawyers and accountants, I was blessed to find partners early in my business career who supported us for the long haul and adapted and evolved to our needs and size. I chose large, full-service law and accounting firms well before I needed them because I expected to have work for them in the future. They came with brand names that were "Googleable" and a scale that was presentable should I need them to interact with a competitor or customer. They weren't the largest, but they were well-respected organizations with internal resources broader than any I needed at the time I selected them (but most of which I would eventually utilize — just like buying an ERP system for the future).

For example, I started working with the law firm of Day Pitney when I needed general business advice. Over the years I used them to litigate legal matters, manage intellectual property initiatives, handle labor issues, draft non-competition agreements, and even do personal legal work. Because I chose the right sized firm, I saved myself the time of having to find a specialist lawyer every time a new project came up. I had signed up for the bigger model and benefited from that when we grew into the need.

GENERAL ADVICE FOR WORKING WITH PROFESSIONALS

Let's say you've done it — you've gone ahead and contracted with a professional resource outside of your own firm, either for the first time or you've upgraded a resource that needed to be shed like a claw. Congratulations! In many ways, however, your work is just beginning. Once you've written a brief and shared it, hold true to what you have put on paper. Here is general advice for getting the most out of your investment:

- When an external resource presents work to you, always start by going back to the brief. Begin giving feedback with something positive. Point out what you like, recognize where your brief or instructions were followed, and compliment and praise. Even

if the work feels wrong, find places where they
listened to you to give credibility for the next phase
of comments when you may challenge aspects
of how they adhered to the terms of the brief.

- If you can start each project with a clearly agreed-
upon and defined plan (in writing), it becomes
easier to be critical down the road. When you
do get to the problems, do not make them
personal issues. It was your job to provide clear
instructions and guidance before any professional
resource got to work. If you documented that in
the form of a brief, you can only criticize them
for failing to work according to the instructions
provided. If you were not clear, it is your fault.

- Never, ever be prescriptive. This applies to your
dealings with all resources, both internal and external.
The moment you step into the shoes of your resource
and tell them exactly how to do their job, you might
as well do the job yourself. You can ask challenging
questions; you can accept blame for failing to provide a
clear-enough brief. You just cannot tell them you want
them to do their job a certain way. That is demoralizing
and takes away the value you are paying for. You
can see the energy sapped from them and you will
get an ever-diminishing return on the investment.

WHAT YOU DON'T NEED

In addition, it is helpful to reflect on what you don't need from
a professional resource. For example, I have always struggled
with the value of consultants who were only there to help

assess a problem and then make a suggestion or proposal, but were not willing to stick around to implement it. That work felt to me like the equivalent of writing a thesis and then placing it on a library shelf to sit and wait for it to be read.

The consultants I hired were not brought on only to give ideas — we always had ideas within our team. They were there to make sure things got done and our ideas were realized. I vividly remember coming into Urnex at 7 a.m. during Will Bachman's first consulting project, only to find him covered in dirt and grease. He'd been on-site for hours and taken it upon himself to change the level of shelves on a twelve-foot-tall pallet rack. He was doing this in order to implement a new factory flow plan he had developed to solve a problem he had identified. The right resources are part of the organization and they contribute in ways like Will did. Find them and your business with benefit.

You also don't need someone constantly trying to prove their worth to you. In the case of lawyers, for example, this is a recipe for a lot of legal fees and a complicated negotiation. I always made it clear to lawyers that I wanted them to protect my interests and to make smart, logical, efficient suggestions about the risks I was taking. I made it clear that changes to a document to say the same thing "our" way were not important to me. Too often, I found that through efforts to demonstrate their value, some lawyers raise small issues. Too many of these have the potential to cause unnecessary distractions. If lawyers are focused instead on protecting your interests in a way that leaves the business side of the relationship or negotiation to the business people, the results are always better.

I was fortunate to have a legal advisor in David Swerdloff of Day Pitney LLP, who recognized my focused desire on getting deals done without extra complications. Over our fifteen-plus-year business relationship (he first represented me on the sale of the lemon cover business when I was consolidating the product lines), David always gave me confidence that I was protected and we were collaboratively moving toward the best outcome possible. We rarely changed language unnecessarily. We may have accepted a few clauses that we didn't like, but we always got the ones that were important. More importantly, we always did so with a reasonable and measured consumption of time and energy and mutual respect.

Finally, it's important to note that we hired all professionals for the long term. However, if the task outgrew a professional resource or they didn't perform the way we needed them to, then we didn't need that either. We let them go like that claw a lobster is willing to abandon to stay alive. *Don't be tied to a decision you've made on an outside resource just because it's a decision you made.* Be confident enough to know when you need to make a change. We must learn from our mistakes to continue on the path of consistent growth, with control for the future.

- **You can't do it alone (second time).**
- **You could do it yourself, but then why did you hire them?**
- **If you don't ask, you'll never know.**
- **Don't be tied to a decision you've made on an outside resource just because it's a decision you made.**

CHAPTER FOURTEEN

AN EXIT OF SCALE

Let me say this as directly as I know how: I strongly, strongly urge you not to run your business with the goal of selling it. You need to approach your business with a long-term sense of ownership and be in it for an indefinite future. Working toward exit is just a distraction from your One Thing. If you do things well, the exit of extraordinary scale will come (if you want it), but if that's your original goal, you may miss the bigger opportunity. Like we said back in Chapter One, don't give yourself an escape hatch; don't use the idea of a future sale to allow you to avoid tough problems (thinking they won't be yours when you sell). A mindset toward exit clouds the decisions about investment and time horizons. If you build a great business, everything else will fall into place. Your options will be diverse and selling will be only one of them.

Just like a lobster, the bigger, stronger, and more profitable your business becomes, the closer you are to eliminating or reducing the vulnerabilities you feel as an independent business owner. You can no longer be caught in a trap (well, you can be caught but the fisherman can't keep you). This mindset of humble strength, knowing traps are out there but being confident in what you are doing, leads to the creation of value. That focus is the difference between a good business and one that is extraordinary. When you get to this point, you will have created your dream job, and by nature, people will want to buy what you've built in hopes of improving it in their own way.

Remember, a sale isn't why we build. We build a business because it can be a fulfilling confirmation of our goals and aspirations. As I said in the opening, building a business can be a chance to create your personal dream job. In reflecting on the philosophies and strategies communicated in the preceding pages, you will recognize that everything is ultimately focused on building an organization that can exist without your presence — that's the source of extraordinary value. In the case of Urnex, the methodical work through molt after molt created value that led to an exit of scale — but an exit was never the goal.

While at times you'll be tired and the idea of selling will creep into the back of your mind, you have to run the business like it is the last job of your life, and selling is not an option. Stay focused and concentrate. Build and follow a clear path to consistent, controlled growth. Soon after, you'll learn that investors unwilling or unable to create what you have will want to participate in your extraordinary results. With 15 percent topline growth (or any number that makes sense for your industry) and comparable or faster increases in profitability, it will all work out fine. Everyone looks for a graph with consistent and smooth trends that move up and to the right. Staying focused and keeping it simple will empower you to create those trends.

ARE YOU READY TO SELL?

Early on, I decided that in order not to be distracted, I was only ever selling the business if the after-tax proceeds made it unnecessary for me to work a regular job again. That was a pretty big ask given where things started. Putting an exit up on such a high pedestal allowed me to appreciate that I had the best job in the world, and gave me a long-term view. Rather than worrying about a sale, I worked hard to make sure that I'd never have to be employed anywhere else. I determined to do all I could to keep strengthening the business and planning and preparing for every successive molt. If the business were not large enough for someone to buy it for what seemed like an unattainable number, I was happy continuing to run and grow it, taking a healthy salary each year. In some ways, setting an aggressive goal of "I never have to work again" allowed me to stay focused on just growing. As I always said to my employees and now I say to my kids: *If we don't set big goals, we'll never achieve them.*

How much does one need to feel totally secure? You can use a number of formulas to determine how much money you need to have in the bank to cover your lifestyle for the rest of your life, based on simple returns and age and your "burn rate." Financial planners and advisors do this for a living. I consulted advisors and approached friends in an effort to rough out what I thought the number was, and then decided that I only wanted a sale if it was even bigger than those calculations. Someone was going to have to really entice me to leave this job.

There are other reasons to time the sale of a business, of course. Sometimes you might be motivated to sell when your business is at a peak ... and before the next dip comes and compromises the marketing "story" of your business. (We'll discuss telling the story of your business further on in this chapter.) At other times, you're

getting older and tired, or your health causes you to rethink things.

In my case, I'd be lying if I didn't admit that my heart scare made me much more keenly aware of my own mortality and opened my eyes to an appreciation of the present and preparation for the future. However, it might surprise you that it wasn't the upside sale price potential and the idea of a financial windfall that motivated me. Rather, it was the risk profile and sort of shell-less vulnerability of what I had to lose if the trend we had been delivering in terms of top- and bottom-line growth one day changed course and a decline happened. At the point I got serious about selling, I was the sole owner, and most of my personal net worth was tied up in the business. I started thinking about a sale or taking on an investor as a way to de-risk. I began to think about an exit to relieve myself of pressure and nourish myself in a healthier way. I was looking for a way to harden my own personal shell.

CONTROL THE PROCESS

Make sure that your decision to sell is a proactive one. No one wants to have to sell because they need to — just like we don't like to look for a job when we don't have one. When the sale closed and I told customers that I had sold the business, they were pleased for me, but many of them running small businesses of their own said the same thing: "So you finally took the call?" I realized then that most business owners are approached every now and then by a broker or small investor looking to buy them, offering them financing, or just hoping to learn enough about them to see if they can sell them something unrelated.

Those inexperienced in the sale of a business had a hard time understanding that just like everything else I'd done in the business, the sale was a deeply contemplated, organized, and discipline pursuit.

It never occurred to me to take *the call* because those unsolicited approaches are distractions from your One Thing. Taking *the call* is about being reactive and not thinking about what you want first.

In the next section, I will step you through the concept of EBITDA, which is an acronym that represents earnings before interest, taxes, depreciation, and amortization. It is at the heart of managing a sale proactively and understanding things on your own terms in a vocabulary that the rest of the world will also understand. EBITDA is a concept that most of you know intimately. Bear with me here when I lay it out in a simple way for a specific purpose: I do not expect that I will teach most of the readers of this book anything about finance, but I do hope each reader will pull out a new way to think about business valuation. Being aware of your financial situation is a way to control the dialogue and know when it is time to think about selling.

Each year (and truthfully at any given moment), a well-run business should be aware of what its EBITDA looks like. You need a sense of what your value might be to a potential acquirer so that you can track your own progress on a universal standard and measure yourself. I tell you this now because while I was aware of the importance of EBITDA in a business valuation, I didn't really start running my business with EBITDA in mind until a year before sale. Had I been more disciplined in my EBITDA management and reporting, I could have increased my purchase price significantly and possibly managed my team differently. I'm in no way regretful of how I ran the business, as the time I might have dedicated to increasing EBITDA in the financial statements would have distracted me from other benefits to the business or my personal happiness (health, family, etc.). But it is good to come to grips with this concept early in your thinking about when the right time to sell might be.

EBITDA

Many of you reading this may consider what follows to be basic information. Yet, for many successful entrepreneurs, financial management is not a skill set. I was quick with the numbers but I never focused on them at the expense of the softer parts of the business, such as people and customers. If you are a private equity investor, a financial advisor, an accountant, or any of a number of other professionals, you should realize that not everyone who is successful in running a business is fluent in financial terms. Many leaders who have focused on running and building a business have less of a need to think about this stuff than you might imagine.

I feel compelled to acknowledge that this book has been light on the topic of finance and accounting. If finance is not your strength, look back to Chapters Seven and Thirteen and be sure you find resources that can ensure your measurement systems are in order. Make the investment of your own time to elevate your understanding of the numbers. They are a tool essential to success. Potential investors value a business in many ways (see *Chapter Ten: Know Your Audience: Competitors*). Here, I summarize the most simple and common ways of using a financial vocabulary that can be understood by a broad range of audiences. Your business value is tied to the story you tell about why you are special. The financial story has its own language but it is still storytelling just like other elements of your business. At a minimum, you need three years of really good information, but five or more makes things more interesting. Most everyone is going to look at EBITDA in some form or another. To be in control of the value you are creating, it might help to dig into this acronym more thoroughly.

- *Earnings:* This is the biggest number and basically what you have left over after your sales are recorded and the cost of goods, advertising, rent, employee compensation, and other general expenses are deducted. It is net profit. The calculated EBITDA is a profit figure that gives you credit for other expenses that are accounting-related and were originally deducted from your earnings. As a result, the letter "E" is followed by ...

- *Before:* This means what you think it means. We're talking about adding back the stuff previously deducted from your profit or earnings. The idea is that things taken away before are returned in an effort to equivalize the value of a business regardless of its tax or accounting practices.

- *Interest:* This is the money you pay lenders on any debt you've used to grow the business. Potential investors don't want to see the cost of loans in the earnings they look at to value your business. This is because most business people assume the debt will go away at the time of the sale. This means that using debt is not necessarily bad for increasing the value of your business, as you can borrow as much as you like and pay lots of interest without reducing your EBITDA. While smart use of debt might help you increase the value of your business, too much debt carries other problems.

- *Taxes:* Similar to interest, potential buyers don't care about your tax bill. Not everyone pays taxes on business income in the same way, since some people own their business as a C-corporation and others in a variety of other legal entities that pass business income to personal tax returns. By excluding taxes from their impact on your business's cash generation ability, you start to get a clearer picture of how your business compares to others.

- *Depreciation:* Depreciation is the accounting expense you include on your financial reports to show the cost of a reduction/depreciation in the value of the capital assets you have purchased in the past. These are assets you acquired to run your business for several years. As a result, we don't count their expenses against the business in the year they were purchased. Depreciation goes up or down depending on your tax or accounting status and the intensity of the types of capital purchases you make. By excluding depreciation from a business valuation model, you equivalize things so that a potential buyer can compare your company's inner value in a vocabulary similar to that of other companies.
  Note: What is interesting about having fluency in explaining depreciation is that you can use it to help your team make better decisions about investments like buying a new machine (depreciable expense) vs. hiring a few more permanent employees (recurring expense).

- *Amortization:* This is much like depreciation, but represents the year-on-year expense and therefore reduction in your earnings by the decline in value of non-tangible purchases or creations. These might include a trademark or a logo that you bought or the brand value of a competitor recently acquired. In my case, the acquisition of worthy competitor Puro Caff brought along *goodwill,* which is an accounting term for the intangible value of what we acquired, like a brand name and logo. Since not everyone records these values in the same way and most of them are driven by tax law, the amortization expense you experience is added back to your profits in calculating your EBITDA.

- *Add-Backs...* Although it is not technically in the EBITDA acronym, you have a chance to increase your EBITDA for valuation purposes by keeping good records or making assumptions about expenses the business pays for that you benefit from personally or that are not related to the normal course of business (such as money spent exploring a new market which you have not yet entered). These add-backs are expenses that the business will not be responsible for after you sell and are probably only expenses to the business because it is privately owned. I'm not saying that the business should be paying for your personal expenses, but there are certainly things that small-business owners benefit from related to their businesses that reduce earnings. These can be added back to the final EBITDA number for sale valuation purposes. Paying for your cell phone (a phone that a buyer won't have to pay for after you leave), the dedicated high-speed internet service in your home office, and the business lease on a car are examples.

The EBITDA is one important measure of what you're building in a business. Of course, you have to think about your working capital (the funds available to fuel the business), cash flow, and the capital expenses required to allow your business to continue to grow. The financial picture of your business is the value you're creating and the shell you are hardening each time you molt. And while it is not the only record that potential acquirers look at, it will be at the centerpiece of their investigative efforts into your business and evaluation of its attractiveness. Understanding it can deliver enormous value.

KNOW YOUR AUDIENCE, FINAL EDITION: YOUR ACQUIRER

There is no question that the sale and marketing of a business are just like the sale and marketing of products or services, and the hiring and recruiting of the top talent you need to accomplish your goals. It all begins with "knowing your audience." Depending on your size, market, and profitability, you must learn who would be interested in partnering with your business and buying or investing alongside you. Will the scale you've achieved be worth more to certain competitors than to those in unrelated businesses? Are you of a size that private equity firms will find interesting? Is there a perfect strategic buyer or a competitor who you've known a long time and who loves your business as a complement to his or her own? Do you have one or more employees who are up to the job and might want to take over from you? There are ways to do a sale to your management team that you can and should consider.

In short, you have a lot of options about who might want to buy your business or invest in it. The types of buyers or investors change with your size. For very small businesses, it is hard to find someone interested in buying because it takes almost the same amount of work to buy a small business as it does a large one.[8] The buyers must investigate every aspect and follow a "due diligence" process beginning with an assessment of your EBITDA and business plan, but not ending there by any means. The effort and expense to learn about a business are similar no matter the size of the business. If the costs involved in this process make the potential return on the investment too low, certain buyers will not be interested — hence the reason some companies only look at acquisitions larger than a certain size.

YOUR PITCH BOOK

In Chapter Nine, we discussed the idea of documenting your job through a business plan, marketing plan, and project/creative brief. Such documents are important for how you run your business — and when it's time to sell, those documents can be easily adapted as tools to market the business. Your pitch book is a snapshot of who you are and it's a great way to help potential investors or acquirers appreciate what you have created. Think of a pitch book as a masterpiece of marketing collateral designed to tell the story of your business. It should include your market size, strengths, priorities, competitive set, and all your financial results and objectives. In essence, it is the articulation of your One Thing and everything you've created to support the achievement of your goals.

As just discussed in Chapter Thirteen, while there are professionals who prepare these documents for a living, you should write your own first draft. You know your business better than anyone and letting someone try to tell your story is going to waste a lot of your

---

8 There is a lot of ambiguity and secrecy about business size and valuation. "How big do you have to be to sell to a private equity firm?" is a question a lot of people ask but few ever answer. Here's a simple rule of thumb. Until the EBITDA of your business passes $3–$5 million, you are probably too small for sophisticated equity investors. There are always going to be players willing to invest at all stages of a business's life, but $5 million always seemed like the place where it gets serious. As you grow, every incremental $5 million and then $10 million of annual EBITDA seems to open up the universe of who will be interested in your business and where you can go for investments.

time when you need to rewrite it. Before I contacted an investment banker or talked to a potential acquirer, I compiled a fifty-page book on the business for the bankers and potential buyers of the business.

Strangely enough, this exercise was as much for me as it was for a potential investor or banker. It gave me a fresh sense of the business and allowed me to put on my consumer-behavior hat and think about how a potential acquirer would look at the business given all the information assembled. It all again comes back to knowing your audience. Here is what we included in the document. Look closely and you'll notice that much of the work was adapted from the business plan:

1. The company's history, story, and market position. I started with what was on our website and expounded.

2. Simple financials showing a growth trend for the last three years. I picked my time frame to show an attractive picture of the trend and then used that trend to build a forecast beyond the current year to paint a picture of where the business was going. Again, this was already available as part of our ongoing tracking efforts.

3. A list of our top twenty-five customers and their sales as a percentage of the total. Buyers are going to be afraid of having only one or two customers that account for a significant portion of your business. They like a smooth business with few big risks and limited customer concentration. If you're measuring your customers, this list is part of your day-to-day management tool.

4. A list of our top five countries and sales as a percent of the total was important because of our global

presence. Here again, we had worked to build a business with a lot of protections and security that were not overly dependent on one market or customer. This business philosophy of building your shell for security was aligned with what appeals to buyers.

5. A breakdown of profitability by customer type and sales by customer type and product line. This demonstrates that you know your business and gives them a good image of your position in the market. If you're running a good business, you should know this as a manager.

6. A breakdown of sales between retail and commercial (or whatever channels you work in), showing a trend in both. What else is specific to your business that you'd want to know if you were the acquirer?

7. Tell the story of the management team: who they are, their background, and profile. Have you built an impressive team? Use that to present your organization favorably. The goal here is to give the acquirer confidence that it's not a one-man or one-woman show, but a viable entity. Share your org chart and all the positions you dream of filling — Think Bigger.

8. Define staffing goals and initiatives. This gives the potential buyer a sense of the easy things still left to be done in your business. It gives them an idea of the places they can add value and get a return on their investment sooner.

9. List the three biggest opportunities for the future and explain the potential. Just like in marketing a product, you need to show the buyer that the future is bright.

10. If you have production equipment or other capital, talk about the plant and age of equipment and recent investments as a way to both instill confidence and give hope for areas to create even more value.

11. Define other investments needed so you are upfront and so they understand they are dealing with a professional. Buyers like to know you are proud of your business but they also like to know you have things you'd like to improve.

12. And finally, include anything else relevant to your business (risks, too) that you would want to know if you were buying it. Full disclosure here is always best.

HIRING AN ADVISOR

Once you cross your own financial threshold for when a sale makes sense, your next step is to reach out to your network of peers, professional service providers, and friends to find an advisor to help you. I asked my lawyers, accountants, and anyone I could think of who might be in the industry for names of bankers, brokers, entrepreneurs, and just about anyone and anything in between. I was determined to get a sense of my options and the approaches I might consider. Talking to people who have sold a business or those who are experts in the field of selling businesses is of the highest importance. Be aware of what you know and what you don't and find the resources that can help you.

I went through a well-conceived selection process to hire an advisor. I decided I wanted to hire an advisor and/or investment banker to lead me through my sale because I wanted to control the message and find the buyer that was right for me, for my business, and for the continuity of my employees. I was not going to react to *the call*.

I knew more about investment banking than most people running a similar company because of my previous employment experience in the field, but I also was aware that this was no longer my expertise. I realized that if we were to sell to a private equity firm, we'd be negotiating with people who do deals eight or ten times per year. I would be a deer in the headlights confronting experienced professionals, and I needed a savvy advisor to help me cross the road. I was only planning to sell the company once, and as a result, I needed support that was aware of the other side and the challenges and tricks ahead of me.

Depending on the size of your business, you might not want to use an advisor because they cost a lot and that is a cut of the pool of money you would otherwise be building to get to your "I don't have to work again" number. In my case, I was only selling if I received that substantial payout after expenses, so I realized that an advisor was imperative and that I'd be able to afford them. It is interesting that the price you pay an advisor is a commission when the sale is completed (if you negotiate the right kind of fee deal). As a result, I had no problem hiring a higher-priced resource since I knew in my head that I didn't have to sell. If the price after paying for services didn't reach my expectations, I was more than happy to just keep running the business until we were ready and able to get my number. While it would consume a lot of time and resources, I was not obligated to pay an advisor fee unless they sold the business. I was not obligated to sell the business for any price I did not find acceptable.

When it came to hiring an advisor, I went on a few criteria: experience in our industry, personal fit with the professionals, attention I would receive from the people I was hiring to work on the deal, anticipated price, and lastly but most importantly, the perception the advisor's name on the offering plan would provide to a potential buyer. Here, I chose the advisor with what I thought was the most prestigious brand identity because I felt that the name of the investment bank lent legitimacy to my deal. I still had insecurity about how my business would be perceived (remember, it was a boring industry by choice), but by working with the right advisor, their great name in the business brought investor interest that otherwise we would not have been able to attract. It all goes back to knowing the audience and presenting yourself as you hope and aspire to be perceived (and to the level you will achieve). In picking an investment banker, we picked a brand that helped Urnex by association. The investment bank was R.W. Baird in Chicago. The end result confirmed this choice was the right one.

Just as I did not start working at Urnex knowing I would sell it, I also did not set out to write a book about how to build a business in order to sell it. While the long-term vision gave me an inkling that I might want to create something I could one day sell, that was not what motivated the actions I took or the decisions I made over the years. I just wanted to build a business I could be proud of and one I enjoyed going to work at each day. I wanted to create true value that gave me a substantial, regular, secure income, and more importantly, gave me the freedom and flexibility to make my own mistakes.

Business, and more specifically independent, entrepreneurial business, is about building yourself a protective shell of resources and support so that you can be free to go out into the wild and explore and develop and challenge yourself and your mind. Being aware of the ups and downs of a business, the molts and hardenings, is the first step in planning and preparing yourself and your organization for future growth and extraordinary success. By doing that, you also make your organization more valuable to others.

(• **If we don't set big goals, we'll never achieve them.**

EPILOGUE AND ACKNOWLEDGMENTS

EPILOGUE

On April 16, 2015, Cortec Group and Urnex Brands closed on a transaction in which a majority interest in the business was sold. Just over fifteen years and five months after I joined, a member of my family was no longer the controlling owner of the company that was founded generations earlier. We had grown an annual average of 15 percent or more since I started. We were mature and had become the clear global market leader of our industry. Most importantly, we worked as a team, aligned in our focus, and always excited to take on every new challenge together. We had created a foundation worthy of another eighty years of survival.

The moment the wire transfer of the sale price hit my bank account and I logged in to see that it was all real, I felt an enormous pressure lifted off my shoulders. It was a sunny day and I walked outside my office in Elmsford, New York, sat down on a tree stump in the grass where I had often taken my dog on walks, and cried. My diary entry that evening read: "It's a feeling I don't really know how to describe. It's part scary, part satisfying, part overwhelming, and part just incredible."

After closing, I chose to stay on as CEO and work with my new partners. I was excited to see what it was like to work with these experienced professionals and I was ready to learn and again have a chance to make new mistakes. The enthusiasm, energy, experience, and perspective of the private equity team were invigorating. The relief of not being the sole and final decision-maker with all responsibility was uplifting. I knew I had created the "best job in the world" for me and I was excited to continue to do it in this new situation. However, I also had a chance to reflect on where I was and look hard at all around me.

While I had not a single complaint working with the new

investors, a few months after the transaction, I realized that I had accomplished many of my early goals. We had achieved a scale that we aspired to and the world could really see us as the company I always expected us to become. As in many of the decisions I made in building and developing the business, I thought hard about myself and my family. I engaged in another process of "knowing my audience." While recognizing our family's stage in life, our newfound financial security, and the opportunities ahead, my wife and I decided this was a new chance to continue to grow.

Fifteen months after the deal closed, I stepped down as the CEO and transitioned to the role of Chairman of the Board. My partners were supportive and deeply respectful of the decision I had made. They wanted me to continue to be involved and bent over backward to make it work for me to stay involved at the Board level.

With confidence that the decision was the right one, my family and I moved into a new house that we now consider home in Florence, Italy. When we arrived, we spoke no Italian, had no Italian ancestry, and knew no one in town other than our realtor and new landlord. We started over with a clean slate in a new country. We had made it through our most recent molts and grown up just a little bit more. When we arrived in Italy, we were sporting fresh, hard shells and ready for the next adventure.

ACKNOWLEDGMENTS

Writing a book is a long and solitary journey. While it may lack the type of satisfaction I found in capturing new sales contracts, implementing well-conceived efficiency projects, or reaching new daily production goals, it does allow for deep reflection. I'm honored to share my story and the insights I've gathered along the way, and grateful to those who have provided inspiration and guidance to me.

Writing *Grow Like a Lobster* has reminded me that as CEO of Urnex, I had the greatest job in the world — my dream job. Every day, I had the chance to work with a talented team of people, and together, we built an amazing brand and organization. To the employees of Urnex and the thousands of customers and friends in the coffee industry around the world, I say thank you for letting me be a part of an amazing community.

When it came to the writing, my friends and colleagues guided me to new sources, read my drafts, and challenged my thinking. Thanks to those who helped me learn about lobsters and those who read and commented on the early drafts, including but not limited to: Will Bachman, Terence Barry, Nils Erichsen, Brad Gibbs, Warren Heffelfinger, Stuart Horwitz, Ben Hoskins, David Schnadig, Professor Michael Tlusty, Todd Tracey, and most of all, my wife, Kristin. She read this over and over and always gave insightful, supportive, and practical advice.

I would be remiss in not thanking Harry, Emanuel, Joey, and Jason Dick. Each contributed something amazing to the business before I ever considered joining. They proved that family businesses can twist and turn and sustain for generation upon generation. I am forever grateful for having had the opportunity to put my mark on something started and nurtured by each of them.

Throughout my journey, my family has been an inspiration. Kristin,

Katherine, Olivia, and Georgia have motivated me to tell my story and share my insights and ideas. I hope each of my daughters will take a little concept or a simple idea from this book and use it to discover her own dream job. Today, I am blessed to be enjoying and experiencing my second dream job, that of a life in partnership with those I love.

APPENDICES

APPENDIX A: MISSION AND VALUES STATEMENTS

MISSION: OBJECTIVE OF YOUR BUSINESS — (WHAT YOU ARE GOING TO DO)

- To make and sell products that fill specialty market needs.
- To offer quality products that satisfy and impress customers.
- To deliver customers the opportunity to enjoy high resale margins.
- To offer employees an attractive lifestyle opportunity.
- To be profitable above and beyond conventional measures.

What does all of that mean? Let's take a closer look:

To make and sell products that fill specialty market needs ...

As far as the first line goes, we always wanted to try and make stuff — but not just any stuff. We wanted to sell items that people wanted to pay a premium for. We didn't specifically reference coffee as that would have been too limiting, but we did identify that we wanted to serve specialty markets, which remains a key descriptor in the coffee industry today. While some businesses thrive in commodities, we weren't going to do that. Personally, and this is important to understand, I like making special things of value (not commodities). I grew up around factories and somehow always liked doing things with my hands. That makes me happy and that's why we started with this statement and included the word "make." In crafting your mission, be sure it includes aspects you enjoy. You are going to spend more of your non-sleeping time running your business and with your team, than you will with family and friends. Steer it in a direction that will make you happy.

To offer quality products that satisfy and impress customers ...

The way this was written, we defined the standard of quality by how our customers would receive our product. This was the first step in a customer-focused business concept. The language was tempered to the level of quality by tying it to the standards of satisfying and impressing our customers. Everyone knows there are cost/benefit trade-offs of quality. If the quality met the expectations and our service impressed our customers, we were doing a good job. I always strived to elevate quality, but most businesses need to do so with a sense of practicality. This statement helped accomplish that balance and avoided distractions. Did we need to invest to reach the next level of quality or was our present product quality level acceptable? For us, this line in the mission statement was where I went to get comfortable with decisions about what constituted acceptable quality. As a perfectionist, having a statement like this gave me the freedom to loosen up a bit and make smart, efficient decisions that were right for the business.

To deliver customers the opportunity to enjoy high resale margins ...

The next point might have been the most important in our business philosophy as it indicated and supported a long-term mindset. I firmly believe in keeping customers happy. Because we were a wholesale or business-to-business model, our customers would want to work with us because the products we provided helped them in many ways. By giving them something they could sell for a high resale (or use to increase or improve their business's operating margins) we found a core to the business model. To put it in context, a popular item sold by Urnex to distributors had a list price of $4 per unit. The standard end user resale price of this item by a regional distributor is over $12. That was a pretty compelling margin offered for our customers to enjoy. Helping customers (mostly resellers) enjoy strong margins allowed us to sell to bigger companies who would, in turn, find volume for us and help make up for our limited sales resources. This philosophy made sure that we never sought the short-term, easy win in exchange for a long-term sacrifice.

To offer employees an attractive lifestyle opportunity ...

This point has the closest overlap with the values statement, which comes next. While leaders and those who are self-employed have ownership of their decisions, such autonomy can be extended throughout an organization in many important ways. To me, one of the best parts of my father running his own business was the fact that he was able to leave the office early enough to coach Little League. I appreciated that and wanted to be able to offer that to my entire staff. In addition, I wanted a lifestyle that appreciates the freedom to take chances, be accountable, and make decisions. It is also one that is understanding, realistic, and positive. As I said in the introduction, I set out to create a dream job that made me happy, and this part of the mission helped make sure that was never forgotten.

To be profitable above and beyond conventional measures ...

Of course, an employee's lifestyle is also influenced by profitability. If you don't make money (unless you're a non-profit), you won't be around a long time. I was never interested in being in the business of just getting by. I aspired to be better than the norm and this language kept the bar high but with room for interpretation. By being profitable, we had a model that helped us grow and add great people who kept on helping us create value. What are your profitability goals? Does your business model permit a similar statement or will you have to think about how to measure your own success in a different way?

VALUES: WHAT IS IMPORTANT TO YOUR BUSINESS AND YOUR ORGANIZATION (HOW YOU ARE GOING TO DO IT)

- Act with honesty, integrity, reliability, and consideration for people and the world.
- Serve our customers as we would like to be served.
- Communicate above expectations.
- Plan and prepare for the future.
- Deliver value for shareholders, employees, customers, and the community.
- Avoid waste. (Added 2008)

Let's unpack these in turn.

Act with honesty, integrity, reliability, and consideration for people and the world ...

As I mentioned earlier, you need to own your own values and then express them through your business. If you do this well, it can really pay off. This line informed the way we negotiated with customers, the places we spent money to correct our errors (which led to happy customers who trusted us), the foundation of incredible customer service, and the chance to become a global company. I always hoped to have a global job and somehow this statement made sure the concept was incorporated into the core of our values.

All my life, I wanted a job that forced me to read the newspaper and understand what was going on in the world. I sincerely meant it and talked about it with every employee. This jibed with another personal philosophy: *I like to sleep at night.* I don't believe any short-term gain is worth sacrificing long-term stress or legal or other problems. Shortcuts of honesty, ethics, or integrity are just that and never work in a business with a long-term vision. I would expect that every business has honesty as a value, but does every employee who is not an owner understand how important this value might be? This is very important to me personally and therefore permeated my business thinking. This is not to say that I'm not aggressive. I just always wanted to temper my aggressiveness with reason and consideration for doing the right thing. You will have to make your own decisions about who you are and how you work best.

Serve our customers as we would like to be served ...

A customer-centric organization must have high standards. This standard is worded here as self-reflection. Would you be happy with being treated this way? What would you expect a company to do for you in this situation? I advised my team to ask themselves those questions and then follow up immediately — they didn't have to pause to ask a superior. They were authorized to spend the money if they had to and never to be "penny wise and pound foolish." If you know what's right and how you'd want to be served, then serve the customer that way — even if they don't expect it.

Communicate above expectations ...

There is an intensity to the level of communication that excellence demands, and that can, in turn, surprise and delight your customers. Tell people what's going on before they ask. Anticipate their desires and concerns. Show them you are thinking about them and openly, humbly, share the good and the bad. Give them reason to trust you, and position your organization as professional. You can do all of this through communication. It is in how you share your brand, market your products, handle your crises, and modestly accept praise.

I often explained to our customer service team that the expectations of communication frequency or detail should not be what the customer expects, but what we expect: how we share information amongst ourselves, how fast we respond to each other's emails, and how detailed we can be with our follow-ups. Surprise and delight with communication. This value applies not only to your external audience, but also to your employees and team. If you can anticipate them and communicate above their expectations, you will be well on your way to knowing them and having their trust and confidence. *See Chapter Four: Know Your Audience: Customers.*

Plan and prepare for the future ...

This encompasses many facets of the organization, from internal investments to advertising to great hires and larger buildings. It is also the essence of the lobster metaphor in that we need to plan for the future molt when our shells are hard and strong. It's the reason we should read books like this one and explore continuing education opportunities, attend lecture series on relevant topics, and travel to visit and observe customers, vendors, and trade events.

From the most mundane things like proper inventory control to impressing a new hire with business cards sitting on his/her desk the day they start, there is no reason to wait or ignore things until later. Being ahead of smaller problems can put you in the right mindset to consider larger issues such as thinking through risk and assessing opportunities. Keep a list of the capital investments you might want to make in the future rather than waiting until you need them. Draft an organizational chart with slots for all the positions you one day hope to hire. It is unlikely that you will ever be able to plan and prepare for every situation, but it is certain that each thing you are prepared for will allow you to focus on those that you have not anticipated.

Deliver value for shareholders, employees, customers, and the community ...

This is about making money and the profitability expressed in the mission statement, but also about making something to be proud of that everyone wants to be a part of. Value is a descriptive financial term, but it can be about much more: pride, honesty, respect, and doing the right thing. Value comes in many forms and shapes. It is present in your brand and in your products and the price they command. In the largest sense, everyone is a stakeholder, from the employees who are incorporated into the business and compensated for it, to the customers who were also tied to the business by the high resale profits we helped them make, to the larger community that we served.

Avoid waste...

See Chapter Eight. If I wrote a lot about the concept of avoiding waste here when there is a whole chapter dedicated to it, I'd be wasting your time...

(• **I like to sleep at night.**

APPENDIX B: LOBSTER LEGS

CHAPTER ONE: YOUR ONE THING

- Focus is the key. Simplified focus is the path to consistent, controlled growth.
- Don't give yourself a chance to fail and certainly don't leave yourself an escape hatch.
- Going too fast has just as many risks as going too slowly.

CHAPTER TWO: MISSION AND VALUES

- Saying "no" may be more important than saying yes.
- Wasting time is a waste of time.
- Unless you know where you want to go, you'll never get there.

CHAPTER THREE: THINK BIGGER

- Asking for a second chance is making a big commitment to never ask for a third.
- Buy and invest for the scale you expect to achieve.
- Without a target, you have no way to hit the bullseye.

CHAPTER FOUR: KNOW YOUR AUDIENCE, PART I: CUSTOMERS

- You are not your target audience.

CHAPTER FIVE: CREATE A POWERFUL BRAND

- Without a brand, you are without an identity.

CHAPTER SIX: KNOW YOUR AUDIENCE, PART II: EMPLOYEES

- You can't do it alone.

- If you don't try, you will never succeed.
- Without having a goal, you'll never reach it.

CHAPTER SEVEN: MOLTING PAINS: PEOPLE

- Look forward, not back.

CHAPTER EIGHT: AVOID WASTE

- The waiting time is the wasted time.
- No one should have to wait for you.

CHAPTER NINE: DOCUMENT YOUR JOB

- When you're moving fast, you have to be sure you don't make a wrong turn.
- Simply put, if we don't set goals, we won't achieve them.

CHAPTER TEN: KNOW YOUR AUDIENCE: COMPETITORS

- If it were easy, everyone would do it.

CHAPTER ELEVEN: GOING GLOBAL: EXPAND YOUR MARKETS

- The most important customers are the ones you already have.

CHAPTER TWELVE: MOLTING PAINS: FACE YOUR CRISIS

- Problems don't go away until we find solutions.
- Mistakes are okay as long as we don't make the same mistakes more than once.

CHAPTER THIRTEEN: OUTSIDE RESOURCES

- You can't do it alone (second time).
- You could do it yourself, but then why did you hire them?
- If you don't ask, you'll never know.
- Don't be tied to a decision you've made on an outside

(resource just because it's a decision

)   you made.

CHAPTER FOURTEEN: AN EXIT OF SCALE

)   ·   If we don't set big goals, we'll never achieve them.

APPENDIX A: MISSION AND VALUES

(·   I like to sleep at night.

NOTES

i   Trevor Corson, *The Secret Life of Lobsters* (Harper Collins, 2004), 35.

ii   Dan Cabot, *"Life cycle of a lobster,"* Lobster Institute, University of Maine, mvtimes.com, July 8, 2010, accessed 2019, https://www.mvtimes. com/2010/07/08/life-cycle-lobster-1446/, https://umaine.edu/lobsterinstitute/.

iii   Trevor Corson, *The Secret Life of Lobsters* (Harper Collins, 2004), 89.

iv   English Oxford Living Dictionaries, undated, https://en.oxforddictionaries.com/definition/psychographics.

v   Mark Kalaygian, *"PetSmart, Petco Losing Ground to Independents,"* PetBusiness.com, Feb. 26, 2019, http://www.petbusiness.com/PetSmart-Petco-Losing-Ground-to-Independents/.

vi   E. Jerome McCarthy, *Basic Marketing: A Managerial Approach* (R.D. Irwin, 1960).

vii   "Before & After: Urnex," *TheDieline.com,* March 26, 2010, https://thedieline.com/blog/2010/3/26/before-after-urnex.html.

viii   State of Maine, Department of Marine Resources Code, Title 12, Section 6431.

ix   Simon and Garfunkel, *"The Sound of Silence,"* 1964.

x   Emily Price, *"Samsung Will Make $110 for Every iPhone X Sold,"* Fortune.com, Oct. 4, 2017, http://fortune.com/2017/10/04/samsung-apple-profits-iphonex/.

xi   Trevor Corson, *The Secret Life of Lobsters* (Harper Collins, 2004), 36.

xii   Heather Ward, *"Specialty Coffee Shops: Market Size in the U.S.," ScanNews.coffee,* Dec. 6, 2016, https://scanews.coffee/2016/12/06/specialty-coffee-shops-market-size-in-the-u-s/.

Made in the USA
Middletown, DE
06 June 2021

41030433R00129